Holistic Entrepreneurs
in China

A Handbook on the World Trade Organization
and
New Opportunities for Christians

Holistic Entrepreneurs in China

A Handbook on the World Trade Organization and New Opportunities for Christians

Kim-kwong Chan
and
Tetsunao Yamamori

WILLIAM CAREY INTERNATIONAL UNIVERSITY PRESS

Pasadena, California

Cover design by Rachel Snodderly

Published by
WILLIAM CAREY INTERNATIONAL UNIVERSITY PRESS
1539 E. Howard St.
Pasadena, California 91114

ISBN 0-86585-002-X

Printed in the United States of America

About the Authors

KIM-KWONG CHAN (PhD, ThD) is Executive Secretary for Mission and Pastoral Formation of the Hong Kong Christian Council and Senior Research Associate, Graduate School of Business, Regent University, Virginia Beach, Virginia. He has authored and co-authored eight books. Among his books are *Protestantism in Contemporary China* (Cambridge University Press, 1993) with Alan Hunter and *Witnesses to Power: Stories of God's Quiet Work in a Changing China* (Paternoster, 2000) with Tetsunao Yamamori.

TETSUNAO YAMAMORI (PhD) is President Emeritus of Food for the Hungry International. He served FHI for 20 years, the last 17 years as its President. Currently he is Distinguished Professor at the Graduate School of Business, Regent University. Prior to joining FHI, he held various academic positions in several colleges and universities in the United States, the United Kingdom, and Japan. He also serves as Visiting Professor in the Department of Ethnology at Central University of Nationalities in Beijing, China, Adjunct Professor of Sociology at Arizona State University, and Senior Research Fellow at the Center for Religion and Civic Culture, University of Southern California. He is author or editor of 19 books.

Contents

Foreword

John D. Beckett

Many, if not most, people employed in the United States are working for the weekends. Their primary fulfillment and sense of purpose come not from their jobs, but from recreational pursuits, family, osr hobbies. Christians are not exempt, often because they have misunderstood God's concept of work.

The error is rooted in dualism, an idea that traces back to Greek culture. We divide our lives into two categories: sacred and secular. Sacred activities might include sharing our faith, reading the Bible, or singing in a church choir. But our everyday work is generally viewed as common or less noble. Consciously or not, we hold so-called sacred activities in higher regard than secular ones. The sad result of this thinking is that our work often signifies little more than a paycheck. Work, so debased, often leads to a lack of morality in business and industry. Some Christian business people put a veneer of religiosity on their essentially secular enterprises, but they're missing a wonderful, life-changing reality—that our work can be our calling in God.

I'm a good example. For years I struggled to understand how to integrate my faith into the rough and tumble, highly stressful world of work. But the buffeting of business problems, which prompted much personal reflection and prayer, finally enabled me to see the simple truth that all of life—including work—is sacred before God and is to be offered back to him.

Our company, the R.W. Beckett Corporation, has become a kind of laboratory, embracing in practical ways the idea that running a company according to biblical truth is not only good theology, but good business. When I took over the firm after my father's death nearly four decades ago, we were a small, struggling company. Today, our privately held business has become North America's largest manufacturer of residential oil burners. With affiliated companies making other products used in the heating industry, we employ more than 500 people. We also formed a separate company, Advent Industries, to provide job training for people who were having trouble finding employment.

A few years ago ABC News profiled our company before a national TV audience, focusing on our approach to combine biblical values with day-to-day work. The hugely positive response to this broadcast convinced me there is a growing grass-roots desire to take work to a higher, more spiritually fulfilling level.

I certainly cannot take credit for our success. God has helped us in big decisions and in small, such as in bringing to us talented and godly employees. These, in turn, have helped us gain new markets for our products, innovate for engineering excellence, and take manufacturing approaches that dignify each person, regardless of their position in the company. God has helped the company to prosper, such that both Christian and non-Christian people have come to admire what he has done in our midst. To him be the glory!

The Beckett Companies have several core values, but the most important is that every person is of infinite worth, an idea that is based on how God views each of us, created in his own image. We give people opportunities to grow and develop their God-given potential through increased responsibilities. We provide incentives to have or adopt children. We pay for continuing education. We insist on our having a profound respect for each individual, not just employees, but all those with whom we do business.

Of course, the volume you are holding is not about a mid-sized business in America, where opportunities to expand are plentiful. This book is about doing business in China—

and how followers of Christ can do it in ways that extend the kingdom of God. It is nearly impossible to do traditional missionary work there. However, an open door exists for entrepreneurs to help China through their skills, capital, and acumen. This most assuredly includes qualified Christians, as well. Yes, Christian business people will be able to influence others with the hope we have in Christ, but they will also provide jobs to those who need them and help develop some desperately poor regions filled with people for whom Christ died. Finally, they will have the chance to impact China's culture with the same biblical values we seek to apply at the BeckettCompanies.

With China's recent entrance into the World Trade Organization, these opportunities will only multiply. *Holistic Entrepreneurs in China* provides clear insights for Christians who want to respond to this new challenge. In the second part of the book you will find thrilling accounts of Christians in China who are making an impact for Christ in various ways. Some are even operating by the same biblical values we've grafted into our business. These men and women have a biblical sense of purpose in their work. They show that the Bible is truly a trans-cultural book, applicable in North America, in China, and everywhere in between. Now, in *Holistic Entrepreneurs*, they provide convincing evidence that when it comes to God's kingdom, there is no divide between sacred and secular. In God's economy, everything—including work—is sacred. This is a great encouragement to me, and I hope to you, too.

Kim-kwong Chan and Ted Yamamori are well qualified to write on this important subject, having shown their generous hearts for China in their first book: *Witnesses to Power: Stories of God's Quiet Work in a Changing China* (Paternoster, 2000). I am confident you are about to see for yourself the wonderful work-world possibilities opening before our very eyes in the great nation of China.

JOHN D. BECKETT
Chairman and CEO
The R.W. Beckett Corporation

Introduction

Proclaiming, "The people of China now stand up," Mao Zedong founded the People's Republic of China on October 1, 1949. Instantly, China became a significant political entity. However, it took 30 more years before China started to become an important economic power, with the reforms of Deng Xiaoping. Today, of course, every major international corporation wants to do business in China. Western political leaders cannot discuss issues in China, such as human rights, without considering their business implications.

With China's December 2001 entry into the World Trade Organization (WTO), that truth has been underscored. WTO membership means that China will have to lower its trade barriers to international businesses. This presents the Middle Kingdom, for the last half-century mired in unworkable socialism, with many challenges and opportunities. The same can be said of Christians, both from China and elsewhere, who seek to influence this vast nation for the kingdom. This volume outlines some of likely results of this historic change and profiles some kingdom-minded businesses in China that may show us a way forward.

Why has China become such a gigantic economic force? First, with more than 1.3 billion potential customers, its sheer size is mind-boggling. These people had almost no disposable income with which to purchase consumer goods just 20 years ago. In that span, however, the country has experienced non-stop annual growth rates higher than 7 percent. China stands alone in this among developing nations over the past two decades. Its Gross National Product has tripled in that time, triggering the appetites of Chinese people for almost every kind of consumer good. The three most popular items in the early 1980s were watches, bicycles, and sewing machines. Today they are cars, houses, and overseas tourism. Total national consumer purchasing power is 20 times higher than before and rising.[1] Since the rate of growth differs from sector to sector and from region to region, almost every kind of good is in demand, from bicycles to cars, from televisions to cell phones. This Chinese craving for consumer goods will certainly be followed by services such as insurance, education, entertainment, and tourism.

The second reason is foreign investment. China trails only the United States as a destination of foreign investment. China's cheap labor, industrious workers, and relatively good transportation and communication infrastructure enable foreign companies to produce quality products for both for export and for China's own consumption. Political stability also bolsters foreign investment. The government has not changed over the past two decades. Its policies encourage steady economic development. Its exports, especially in toys, textiles, and light household appliances, already dominate the world market. China's trade surplus with the United States now outranks Japan's. China enjoys the largest trade surplus with the United States in the world—$83.8 billion in 2000.[2]

Yet the large influx of capital and foreign companies in China radically changes the economic landscape of this nation. Its enormous economic potential is just coming to the fore in the coastal provinces. The vast northwestern regions and their matching natural resources have yet to be touched. Third, China has awakened as an economic power. Seemingly overnight, China has become one of the world's largest markets for nearly every kind of good and service. The business community experienced a kind of euphoria during a stampede to set up businesses from the mid-1980s to the mid-1990s. Today, however, after more than a decade of expensive lessons learned, many executives are more cautious. With the entry of China into the World Trade Organization, executives once again are giddy. To join the WTO, China must end its protectionism and allow international corporations access to nearly all sectors of the economy. This enormous change is similar in scope to the sudden influx of foreign businesses after the Opium War in the mid-19th century.

Seizing this opportunity, many education programs offer special concentrations or courses on doing business in China. Hundreds of books promise to help business people enter the market. Most of them are fairly technical, focusing on the legal aspects of entry or serving as "how to" manuals. There is also a wealth of academic literature on China's business environment. However, few books explore China's complex sociocultural reality. Fewer still examine China's business scene from the perspective of the kingdom of God.

Do Christian business people have anything to contribute, not only economically, but also spiritually? Indeed they do. Often the gospel has followed the merchants in China's history. Sometimes there have been good results from a Christian perspective. Other times the pairing of God and Mammon has been problematic.

Christianity first came to China in the seventh century via Nestorian missionaries who tagged along with Central Asian merchants from Baghdad via the Silk Road. Several centuries later, Marco Polo established a trading link from Europe, and the Franciscans later followed a similar route to China. In the 16th century, Portuguese merchants established a permanent trading post, Macao, in China. The Jesuits benefited from this enclave to establish a mission-staging platform to China. Among the many Jesuits who went to China via Macao was Matteo Ricci. Further, merchants in Macao provided continuous financial support to Jesuit missions in China. Without Sino-European trading activities based in Macao, Jesuit missions to China may never have taken off. In the mid-19th century the opium business, and the subsequent battles between China and Western nations, opened China for international trade as well as for missionary activities. Of course, the close relationship between mission and commercial endeavors during this period has rightly been subject to serious moral judgment. Some missionaries serving with the East India Trading Company sold opium to China. Others, serving as translators, misled the Chinese by inserting treaty clauses that favored missionaries. Not surprisingly, resentment toward Westerners and xenophobia were accentuated.

Will the expected opening of China's market introduce more greed and exploitation? Will things perceived to be Western, including Christianity, again be stigmatized and eventually rejected? Or will some of the Christian entrepreneurs see China as a place to advance the values of the kingdom through good business practices? Such an approach is vital in this nation, where missionaries are legally prohibited but business people are welcome. However, Christian business people must first take a hard look at the country's business environment. They must also study its history, culture, politics, and diversity—topics that are not fully treated in conventional business manuals. Now is the time for Christians who can demonstrate holistic entrepreneurship (doing ministry through business), demonstrating God's kingdom in relevant ways to a nation that prohibits traditional mission.

PART ONE:

Foundations

Chapter 1

History

The Chinese are proud of, and yet haunted by, their own history. Historical events shape the collective psyche. For several thousand years, China was an agrarian society in which most people lived off the land. The main objective of Chinese emperors was to sustain this system, and agrarian society was ideal for rule by emperors. Self-sufficient in their small communities, peasants produced all they needed. They lived primitively at a marginal subsistence level and had little disposable income. They also engaged in some bartering, but the circulation of goods, as well as the movement of the people, was limited. There was little flow of commodities and limited circulation of currency. People were tied to the land and had to toil hard to make a meager living. This is a prescription for a tranquil society, composed of numerous powerless communities with little connection.

Trading was discouraged. Large-scale production was not viable. Peasants had no cash with which to buy things. Accordingly, there was little room for commercial activity, and little capital in the private sector to establish any sizable enterprises. The government did little to develop the market or to stimulate economic activity. Therefore, unlike Europe during and after the medieval period, Chinese society did not produce considerable numbers of wealthy middle-class merchants. Even when the Industrial Revolution changed European society from an agrarian-barter market to an industrial capitalistic one, China did not undergo any major changes. China was still perpetuating an ideal—yet poor—agrarian world.

From the mid-16th century onward, China adopted a closed-door policy. It banned foreign trading except for the little undertaken by the government. It created a huge "Forbidden Zone" along the coast to prevent citizens from going overseas for trade or other business, and to protect China from invasion by sea. The rulers believed that overseas territories could become sanctuaries for anti-government political forces. They also knew that Holland and Spain would not be able to invade without a coastal foothold in China.

Further, the emperors always thought of China as the center of the world. (The name China means "the central kingdom.") China has been one of Asia's most powerful empires for centuries. Because of its vast territories, the land generates virtually every kind of product. The emperors believed that China needed no trade with other countries. The needs, of course, were measured by agrarian standards. The relationship between China and its vassal states, such as Korea, Mongolia and Cochin (now Indochina), demonstrate this attitude. These nations gave the Chinese emperor annual tributes of local products. In return, the emperor would bestow lavish gifts of Chinese silk and porcelain, which were worth far more than the value of the tributary gifts. This was not fair trade in the modern sense but a diplomatic power play. China's rulers generally felt that these foreign nations needed the goods of China, not China theirs.[3] The government monopolized foreign trade and treated it as a diplomatic matter. There were no private international trading houses, except for a few licensed by the government.[4]

China's rulers also made sure that business people would not become too powerful. Merchants were at the bottom of the social ladder despite their wealth. Government officers and scholars ranked first, followed by peasants, then craftsmen, and, finally, merchants. Chinese people viewed the merchant class as a group of non-productive people who made profits by defrauding peasants and craftsmen. Scholars described merchants as those who just chased after money and who had no morality or culture. There were even laws from the 15th to the 18th centuries forbidding the merchant class to wear silk, write civil servant exams, or to take positions in government. As the central government became weaker, these rules were gradually relaxed.

The commodities that everyone needed—such as salt and grain—were under the control of the government. The others were supplied by small production units usually run by families, such as neighborhood bakeries and noodle shops. These cottage industries had a limited clientele and scale. They could never become a financial and economic force to threaten the government. Limited demand and rural poverty kept these operations small. If a business grew, the government would curb it. Government intervention and control were the historical norms. There were, of course, exceptions when the political center was weak or on the verge of collapse. But when there was strong political leadership, the government tended to dictate every sphere of life, from religion to trading.

As central government authority weakened in the mid-19th century merchant groups began to emerge. Merchants from Jiangsu monopolized the salt trade. Shanxi merchants specialized in banking and loans. Wenzhou merchants operated most of the pawnshops, and Zhejiang merchants operated in textiles. These informal trade unions elevated the social status of business people. They also enabled merchants to negotiate collectively with government officials. The groups also created platforms for new relationships between the business community and the government. However, the bottom line of these business communities was profit, not sociopolitical reform.

As government power and intervention declined, more government-merchant partnerships developed, and commodities markets began to emerge. As new wealth circulated, it generated even more economic activity. Instead of curbing this process, government officials began to trade their positions for financial gain. Corruption became synonymous with government administration and with business. Gradually, merchant groups began buying off local officials to further their businesses. Flush with wealth, the merchant class lavished gifts on painters, artists, and scholars to gain social acceptance. Many bought or bribed for honorary civil titles to enhance their social status—a situation previously unheard of.

The Opium War had a long-term impact upon subsequent generations of Chinese leadership with regard to international trade. In the late 1700s, the British tried to trade with China, but China sold much more of its goods— primarily tea and silk—to the British than they could sell to China. It was a classic trade surplus for China. British silver poured into China when Chinese goods became fashionable in Europe. Among the many goods China received (such as textiles, pocket watches, and silverware) was opium, which the country imported as medicine. In the early 1800s, opium became China's No. 1 imported item. The East India Trading Company cultivated opium plantations in India to supply this exploding market. Soon China's trade surplus became a trade deficit. Its treasury empty, the government issued a decree banning opium smoking. The decree had no effect. Opium smoking had become a fashionable leisure activity among the royals. Then came a dispute over opium that Chinese authorities had confiscated from British merchants. The British sent in the military. China defended its dignity and sovereignty with a much weaker force and lost the war.

This humiliation forced China to remove its trade restrictions with Western nations. Suddenly, China was flooded by all kinds of goods churned out during the Industrial Revolution. Within a few decades, Western textiles, chemicals, and household goods dominated the market. Traditional household cottage industries could not compete with these foreign products of superior quality. Soon, China's mining, railway, telegraph, and electric power industries were under the control of Westerners. By the 20th century, many international banks, such as Chartered, Indo Suez, and Sakura, were issuing currencies in China, alongside Chinese currency. Pharmaceutical outlets such as Watson's, oil companies such as Mobile, and insurance companies such as AIA all became the leading firms in China in their respective fields. China's economy was at the mercy of these firms until 1950. Chinese merchants either lacked capital and technology or modern corporate governance. While some managed to establish respectable Chinese firms, such as the Sincere retail shops, they were, by and large, too small to make any impact on the economy. Meanwhile, China suffered for the first five decades of the century. No effective government structures existed to protect the fledgling Chinese industrial and commercial capacity. Foreign merchants, however, could do whatever they wanted to exploit this huge market. The local Chinese could not withstand them.

Meanwhile, many Chinese began to harbor anti-foreigner sentiments. The Chinese regarded the Opium War, and the subsequent opening of trade, as a national humiliation. Seeing no help coming from their corrupt government, they lashed out against foreigners whenever they could. Many groups launched patriotic campaigns that called on people to use Chinese-made goods (although often with inferior quality). Boycotts of foreign goods became common. Frustrated mobs even began burning foreign products.

This intense nationalism presented the Chinese Communist Party with a powerful support base, which eventually led to its success. One of its first political moves was nationalizing all industrial and commercial activities. The regime quickly slapped a moratorium on foreign business in China. The communists tried to build up the newly founded People's Republic of China without outside help, with only a brief interlude of support from the Soviet Union. Each time the Chinese made a motorcycle or a watch (to replace those made in the West), it was a time of national celebration. These goods symbolized the long yearning for a strong

China to cleanse itself. The sentiment was that China could produce anything the West could, even the atomic bomb. This pride came with a heavy price tag. From 1950 to 1980, China as a whole believed that it was self-sufficient and did not need to trade with other nations. This worldview resembled that of the Chinese emperors of the past. The communists also asserted that an egalitarian, socialist system provided the best living conditions in the world. They regarded free-market capitalism as an exploitative and enslaving system.

Not until the late 1970s did the senior leadership become aware of the economic and technological chasm between China and the industrialized nations. They then began seeking ways to shrink the gap. Their basic assumption was that China could borrow Western technology and increase economic output without changing the socialist system. This approach somewhat resembled the failed modernization efforts of the Qing Dynasty during the late 19th century.[5] As the government advocated its new Open and Reform Policy of 1980, it became clear that any "reform" would not be allowed to jeopardize the Party. The goal was to catch up with the powerful Western nations so that China could reassert its importance on the international scene. Still embittered against the West, China simply wanted to be a strong and proud nation that could compete with the Western world. This competitive mentality subtly underlines almost all of China's foreign policies as well as its business and economic dealings.

The Chinese always assume that foreigners have come to exploit China. Trade practices that foreigners see as unfair are common in China. Even with the WTO entry, it may take a long time for foreign business people to convince the Chinese that they are not economic invaders. It will be a long time before the Chinese can heal from their national wound.

The Chinese have a win-lose mentality when they deal with foreigners. They think that if one party gains, the other has to lose. China still wants to win back its central position in the international community. This has been a national obsession for the past 150 years. In business negotiations, the Chinese fight for every inch of gain, however trivial. If they can wrest a concession, they believe that they have beaten the foreigner—a symbolic victory for national pride. Chinese leaders rarely accept what Westerners call a "win-win" deal. To present something as such is usually a wasted effort. Smart business people know the symbolic value of a concession, even in win-win proposals.

To "catch up with the West," the Chinese may acquire technologies, goods, or equipment that are not economically practical but are politically significant. Since the advanced nations have something, the reasoning goes, China should as well. Because China is a great nation not to be despised by others, it should be able to produce and own anything the rest of the world has. Otherwise, it is not a great nation. Foreign business people are sometimes surprised to discover that the Chinese import goods or technologies with little relevance to current social needs. Many Chinese markets reflect an urgent attempt to outgrow the historical shadow of an inferiority complex. Many Chinese still equate progress with technological means. This belief prevailed among officials in the Qing Dynasty after the Opium War. It continues among the senior cadres of the current government in Beijing.

For example, the health ministry of a southern province decreed that all hospitals at the county level and above should have a Cathode Scan machine (CAT-scan). Officials, after visiting Hong Kong and the United States, concluded that hospitals in developed countries always have CAT-scan machines. They decided that every bit of the government's health budget would go to CAT-scan machines—regardless of the need. In some rural counties, local hospitals could not even afford an ambulance or a clean operating room. Needless to say, few of the local physicians know how to operate or to maintain these machines. Most are still sitting idly in many hospitals several years after the purchase. However, a government report stated that the hospitals in this region were technologically at par with the hospitals in developed nations—an achievement that resulted in the promotion of several senior officials in that ministry. Many officials genuinely believe they have caught up with the West and proudly show these machines to foreign visitors.

Other examples abound. China prefers to develop its own space program, in effect reinventing the wheel, rather than cooperate with Russia to jointly send astronauts, which would be far cheaper. Entrepreneurs can easily sell obsolete aeronautical technologies to China at a huge profit. The government poured huge sums into the latest broadband technology in Shanghai for all the high schools. This was perhaps one of the most advanced IT educational systems in the world. At the same time, however, hundreds of thousands of rural children cannot get even the most basic primary education. Their parents are unable to pay the annual school tuition of $20. Meanwhile, with millions of citizens living below the absolute poverty line, Beijing has pledged to spend at least $100 billion for the 2008 Olympic Games in 2008. The government provides only meager assistance for poverty alleviation projects. [6] These do not fit into the government's general mentality—to build a "strong nation," at least, in appearances, regardless of the cost. The Chinese simply do not want to be looked down on by the foreigners.

China believes that foreign business people only want to take advantage of the Chinese, while many business people simply want to make fair and legitimate deals. This clash of perceptions can lead to some ethical questions for the sensitive person. Should you sell goods in China if your client may not benefit but your company would? Should you refrain from closing the deal, meaning your competitor gets the contract and you fail to meet your sales quota? It will be a challenge for Christians to discover business opportunities within the framework of kingdom values. Christians face constant ethical challenges related to China's humiliation and psychic wounds.

Chapter 2

Culture

Virtually anyone who does business in China emphasizes the importance of relationships (*guanxi*). *Guanxi* becomes an integrated element of almost every business transaction. To cultivate a good relationship means to develop a positive business foundation. *Guanxi* well nigh dictates the actions of the various business partners on everything from securing a contract to establishing customer loyalty. Relationships are the foundation of Confucianism, which is the basis of Chinese civilization. Relationships are also closely linked to the Chinese social concept of respect, or "face," which may determine the success of a business deal. In the context of relationships, the interests of communities often override the importance of individuals. Further, pragmatic needs often take precedence over ideological or legal considerations. All these cultural elements, which are rather different from those in the Western world, carry significant implications in China's business environment.

Relationship (*Guanxi*)

Confucianism stresses order and relationship. In this system, society is a vast network of interlocking relationships with vertical and horizontal dimensions. There are five basic relations: king and court officers, parent and children, husband and wife, siblings, and friends. Contrary to the American ideal, people are not treated equally, and their behavior depends on the roles they play in particular relational contexts. The type of relationship defines the kind of interaction. For example, court officers are expected to have loyalty to the king, regardless of the king's decisions—even wrong ones. Similarly, the king protects his servants even when they commit mistakes. Relationships override justice. There is no concept of social equality. A general is expected to protect his son using all his political power. In a reciprocal manner, the son obeys his father regardless of the situation. Relationships become a social bond that allows an individual to tap into social resources. A person who has many relationships with the powerful is a resourceful individual—despite the few material goods he may own.

Relationships are a reciprocal dependency that can be cultivated. One may start with a simple friendship with another individual. As time goes by, the relationship deepens through various small gifts and favors. Gradually the other party moves from a peripheral relationship into the person's inner circle. As the relationship deepens, mutual obligation and responsibility are widened. The closer the relationship, the more enmeshed these two individuals become. In fact, Chinese society is an interlocking network, with many undifferentiated bodies connected with each other in various degrees and ways. Through this complex bonding, one can have access to virtually every individual within this network.

The relationship also serves as collateral for any transaction. In lieu of an effective legal framework to protect business transactions, trust becomes vital. In China, one can hardly do any business using the cold-call method, for few would respond to a stranger. The issue is not about what one can offer but who you are. If a person receives an introduction or endorsement from someone known by the firm, the firm may receive him or her. There is an unspoken rule that such an endorser is responsible to intervene should the deal turn sour. In many cases, the endorser is expected to compensate the firm for losses arising from the endorsement. Reciprocally, this endorser may have to accept people, or deals, introduced by this firm at a later time, in a quid pro quo. Although having a good network of relationships with powerful people is a valuable asset, keeping such relationships is a costly affair. Further, using a relationship is always a calculated affair. Eventually there is a price to pay or favor to return.

For example, suppose Chinese firm A wants to do business with foreign firm B. The CEO of the Chinese firm would not consult the phone book or search on the Web for relevant counterparts. Instead, he would approach some business partner C who had dealt with foreign firms. C would introduce B to A, even if B might not be the best partner for such a deal. However, A feels that since C introduced B, then A would trust B because A trusts C. Such trust in relationships is, in the eyes of the Chinese, more important than the legal documents signed by A and B. When B fails to deliver its part, A could take C hostage and demand that C work on B until B fulfills its duty. However, if A and B both profit from this business relationship, C can claim credit and expect to receive some favor from both A and B. C can introduce A or B to other Chinese firms. However, C really has no legal obligation in the deals between A and B.

Relationships are regarded as long-term objectives in any interaction. The Chinese like to build long-term friendships before engaging in cooperative business ventures. After all, the relationship is more important than the success or failure of a couple of joint ventures. Business cooperation is a means to build relationships. Therefore, in any business negotiation, the Chinese parties emphasize the importance of a long-term relationship instead of the short-term gain. Following this logic, the Chinese expend more effort cultivating a friendly relationship than checking over the details in a contract. Business entertainment would be as important as, if not more than, business negotiation. The Chinese would even lose in a business deal just to build a relationship. For example, in the early 1980s, the Chinese purchased a Yugoslav ocean liner that had capsized during her maiden voyage because of bad design and workmanship. China knew this and bought it anyway. Why? To maintain the long-term friendship that China had with Yugoslavia. From a strictly business perspective, it was a bad decision. But from a relationship perspective, it was an excellent decision. With good, long-lasting relationships, anything is possible in China. Without them, it is hard to get anything done.

Respect and Dignity

Respect and dignity are essential within the network of relationships. In Chinese, the concept is called *mianzhi,* or "face." People are not treated equally in a hierarchical social structure. The higher their status, the more respect they receive. Subtle cultural norms govern how one treats individuals and groups. Face dictates that individuals treat their counterparts slightly better than what they would expect in their regular context. It is common to hand out lavish respect in public. This makes the recipient feel that he is high on the social ladder. In return, the recipient honors the other party in various ways, such as by closing a business deal. At a party, one would address a manager as a higher-ranking executive. This is not a lie but protocol.

When dealing with groups, it is important to discover people's rank within the hierarchy and treat them accordingly. Senior leaders expect to be seated in the prominent places and be accompanied by the senior representatives of the counterpart organization. But if they are treated as subordinates, they see this as a deliberate insult and as a reason to break the relationship. All these unseen dynamics occur outside the negotiating room, and yet they may affect a business deal more profoundly than the legal terms spelled out on paper.

Respect paid to the Chinese partner is a glue bonding the two parties. Both parties reinforce their relationship and enhance each other's social status publicly. This elevation in social status adds value to any deal. It can be calculated as part of the profit, at least within the Chinese mindset. A successful deal, in the eyes of the Chinese, may not solely depend on the financial bottom line. There are other gains, such as "face," to consider. It is not uncommon for the Chinese to participate in a business deal that loses money but gains face. For example, a party in Hong Kong had been negotiating with a partner in Guangxi Province for almost a year. Although all seemed to be in order, the China side was holding up the deal. The Hong Kong partner soon realized that the China side was looking for some "face." The Hong Kong leaders decided to make the senior members of the China side feel respected. They arranged an exclusive business trip for them to meet prominent people in Hong Kong. Technically, the junket had nothing to do with the deal. But as the senior people from the China side gained "face" from the trip, they signed the deal. Later, they invited the Hong Kong partners to visit Guangxi officials. According to one of the Hong Kong delegates, this was a total waste of time. Yet in the larger scheme it was necessary. This reciprocity fostered the relationship between the parties, and it has enhanced the social status of the Chinese partners.

In societies where people are not treated equally, one has to tread lightly in arranging receptions for delegates from the same party. If someone takes offense, the whole deal could crash and burn. This kind of hierarchical system is seldom compatible with our modern organizational structures. For example, the local Communist Party secretary may well be the key decision maker for a factory, even though he is nominally just the deputy manager. In fact, the general manager often takes orders from the deputy manager. Therefore, the deputy manager needs to be treated the same as the general manager and seated at the same table. There are other pitfalls the Chinese bureaucratic system has for the uninformed. One of these is the chauffeur. In the West, the chauffeur is not considered part of the negotiating team. However, the chauffeur often sits at the same table and takes charge of the ordering and the paying. He is, in fact, the aide-de-camp of the senior official. If he were excluded from the dining table, the senior official would feel insulted.

In China, government ministries wholly or partly own many businesses. Even "private" enterprises may have to pay tribute. Would-be foreign partners must find out to whom, or to which ministry, an enterprise belongs, and negotiate directly with the relevant ministry. For example, Buddhist organizations operate many vegetarian restaurants in China. The potential business partner in a joint venture is usually not the management staff, or even the local Buddhist organization, but the local government Religious Affairs Bureau. Ministries operate many enterprises with no seeming connection. For example, the Academy of Social Sciences operates a restaurant, a hospital operates a nightclub, the Army operates a fashion boutique, and the Ministry of Agriculture operates banks. It would be wise to find out who is behind an enterprise or a business partner so that proper respect can be paid to relevant officials.

Community over Individual

In the West, the individual defines a community; in the East, or at least in China, the community defines an individual. In China, nearly everyone legally belongs to a social "unit," such as a factory, a company, a school, or a village. The unit takes care of nearly all the individual's needs. To a certain degree, the unit replaces the traditional extended family or clan. Independent existence was almost unknown until recent years. Today, China allows individuals to make their way in society as long as they can do it without state support. (This does not mean that such hardy souls have no safety net. Often they fall back on the traditional family system.) In other words, Chinese people always work not just for their individual needs, but also for their units, whether they are families or companies. In China, family or community needs override individual needs. A community's success naturally translates into pride that all its members can share. The sense of corporate identity is extremely strong.

Following this line of thinking, the community's welfare

naturally supersedes the individual's. For example, a business decision may be considered not only for its benefit to the company but also to the community. Many state owned enterprises (SOEs) are money losers that demand huge government subsidies. From a pure business standpoint, the government should declare them bankrupt. Such action would be legal. However, this step is rarely taken. This reluctance is a major obstacle for economic reform, but it is based on concern for the social consequences of such decisions. Millions of semiskilled, middle-aged workers who had been serving the country through these factories for most of their lives would lose their jobs. Such enterprises are like township governments that provide almost all social services and benefits to employees. While closing the doors of an SOE may make a lot of sense financially, the community would have to absorb the unemployed or underemployed workers with no other place to go. Chinese culture condemns those who legally seek profit for themselves at the expense of the many. Therefore, any joint venture in China must consider community welfare beyond the strictly legal parameters. Businesses, for example, are obligated to provide continuing care for retirees.

Relationships between enterprises in the same field resemble those of members in an extended family. Chinese people always value the family's prosperity and prestige. For example, in the early 1990s, a subsidiary of Guangzhou Ministry of Chemical Industry (GMCI) had invested $25 million in a plant for a specialized chemical. When the factory was under construction, the price for the product, which China imported, was rather high. But just when the plant was completed, the price of the product plunged due to an oversupply and a lack of demand in the international market. Production procedures had changed elsewhere, making the new Chinese plant basically obsolete. It ended up costing the company twice as much to produce the chemical rather than to import it. It would cost the company an additional $20 million to retool the factory for another product, which would have a very uncertain market.

✳ From a business perspective, it would be better simply to write off the plant and fire all 400 employees. However, GMCI decided it would take care of the people for the general welfare of the community. It ordered its most profitable plant, Guangzhou First Chemical Company (GFCC), to absorb this new plant. GFCC would increase its net assets by $25 million, but it would have to buy the chemical at twice the market value and keep 400 more people on its payroll. One of the senior managers said: "This move would wipe out our projected annual profit. However, we are willing to make a sacrifice so that our people can have jobs and we can take pride in our [company's] name." Community welfare is more important than the profit or loss.

In another example of community over efficiency, the government banned direct selling. Companies such as Amway and Avon had entered China in the late 1980s with various degrees of success. Soon many copycat companies arrived, some pushing the legal limits. However, the approach had sparked a growing industry, and many people were making profits with quality products and personal attention. Commercially speaking, the government saw direct marketing as an economic positive, especially with such a huge population just beginning to unleash its economic potential. However, with the emergence of the controversial and secretive Falun Gong, a Buddhist offshoot group, the government decided that social stability is the most important criterion in any policy. Consequently, in April 2000 it banned direct selling. It would not tolerate organizations that it could not monitor, such as the hierarchical structure existing between sales representatives. (The quasi-religious nature of some of these sales rallies was a further concern.) The government's concern for social stability outweighed a potentially profitable industry that would benefit only a few.

Benefit to the community, such as social stability, often overrides individual rights. It is common to promote under-qualified ethnic minority employees to promote harmonious

community relationships. The majority Han Chinese sometimes have to sacrifice their rights. Management cannot rely
solely on performance when evaluating staff. This may not
be fair for some who have performed well and yet have
failed to get promoted. However, the needs of the community are more important than the individual.

Pragmatism

The Chinese people generally are pragmatic. Reasons for
this pragmatism are not hard to find. The government's
white paper on human rights states that people in China
have the right to sufficient food. For centuries, China has
had a huge population and very limited resources. Today, it
has to feed 23 percent of the world's population with just 7
percent of the farmland. The majority of the Chinese, who
are peasants, are happy if they just get enough to eat.
They consider anything beyond subsistence level to be a
luxury. Most of the Chinese are simply following Maslow's
hierarchy of needs. Few have the luxury to care about ideological issues. During most political transitions, people seem
to hope merely for an improvement in their living standards—
a pragmatic goal rather than an ideological aspiration.
People support regimes, whether communist or democratic,
only if they can provide a reasonable living standard.

Except for brief flings with idealistic radicalism (1958–
1961 and 1966–1976), the Chinese Communist Party has
ruled the country rather pragmatically. During its first 10
years of rule, it focused mainly on economic development
and infrastructure building. Immediately after the Cultural
Revolution (1966–1976), the nation returned to a pragmatic
national modernization program. Deng Xiaoping's motto—
"Regardless of the color of the cat, a good cat is the one that
catches the mouse"—became the guiding philosophy of the
"socialist" nation.

The Chinese government officially stresses socialism, an
ideology enshrined in the Constitution, as state orthodoxy.
Chinese people, in general, pay lip service to ideological

matters and behave pragmatically. For example, the government's orthodoxy is atheism. However, to rally religious believers for their contributions to the society, the government tolerates religious activities. It even encourages believers to establish businesses and social services, fully aware that they hold a "distorted and unscientific" worldview that needs to be liberated. Pragmatism clearly overrides ideological purity here.

This pragmatism often leads to an "end justifies the means" mentality. Bypassing legal channels, corruption and smuggling are tolerated—even encouraged—by the business community. The legal system is far from perfect. A huge bureaucracy further complicates legal confusion. Maneuvering through China's maze of bureaucratic and legal challenges is a nightmare for any business.

Complicating matters are the many gray areas. Not surprisingly, few, if any, Chinese business people follow the law. As quickly as legislators can draft new laws, Chinese entrepreneurs find new ways to stretch the limits. In these uncharted waters, pragmatism and common sense overrule legality. Practices seen as illegal in the West are completely acceptable in China. For example, one U.S. firm built a large manufacturing complex in southern China. Although all the papers were signed and the local government welcomed the construction, the company discovered that it faced seemingly endless regulations. No fewer than 27 government offices required applications for approval. Following the letter of the law would have taken at least two years before the ground could even be broken. In the end, the company just paid a public relations firm operated by ex-government cadres to "arrange" everything. This firm was retained after the building was completed to ensure a regular supply of power, water, and police patrols.

One cannot ignore the cultural elements—relationship, dignity, community, and pragmatism—that have shaped Chinese society for thousands of years. Regardless of the regime's stated political aspirations—whether communist, feudalist, or royalist—the leaders are the Chinese who share the same cultural values. These cultural values color business relationships in China. Knowing them allows one to gain valuable insights into the actions and expectations of Chinese business and government entities. On the other hand, not knowing them can lead to needless misinterpretations, wrong responses, and lost business.

How do these cultural values fit into a kingdom scheme for the Christian? Like most other cultural values in any society, these can be a two-edged sword. Used properly, they can make positive contributions to the advancement of the kingdom. Relationships have always been emphasized in the Old Testament. Fostering relationships builds strong community. Common good over individual gain has always been a universal virtue, at least before the rise of Western individualism. This value provides special protection for disadvantaged and marginalized members of communities. Pragmatism, at times, can counterbalance legalism, which sometimes can become extreme. Respect and dignity can enhance personal value and strengthen self-esteem. However, these values, when used improperly, can lead to greed, lies, and other kinds of deception. We need wisdom and critical discernment to integrate these cultural values into kingdom business practices.

Chapter 3

Sociopolitical Dynamics

Politics is both the ideal and the means of governance. In China, it determines the livelihood of the average Chinese, and it plays an important role in shaping the market. For example, the government's one child policy limits, on the one hand, the population of potential young customers. On the other hand, it promotes the sale of expensive, high qualty toys that parents would buy for the only heir When the government launches anti-corruption campaigns, sales of luxury consumer goods drop virtually overnight. When the campaigns are over, all sorts of luxury goods and services reemerge. When Sino-American relations hit a low, such as during the spy plane incident of April 2001, the government promotes Sino-Russian trade. China's market directly responds to current political policies, which in turn influence social life. Because China is rapidly reforming, its business environment faces a bewildering array of new sociopolitical dynamics. The following are some of the more significant ones: political policies, state owned enterprises, economic polarization, and population migration. ✳

Political Policies

China is a one-party state. The Communist Party, by law, r ules China with absolute authority. The Party establishes policies that directly affect the livelihood of all Chinese people. Being the sole decision-maker, the Party decides all socioeconomic policies in accordance with its political

23

objectives, rather than market dynamics. For example, Beijing invested heavily through many front companies in Hong Kong's overheated real estate and stock markets just a few years prior to the 1997 handover. The central government's political objective was to have a smooth transition by gaining economic control. Many ministries and provincial governments established companies in Hong Kong and pumped in capital according to the central government's plan. Needless to say, many of the investments, particularly in real estate, were less than wise. Many of these companies suffered huge losses when the real estate market collapsed just a few months after the handover.

Local leaders can formulate their own policies as long as these are in line with the spirit of central policy. When the central government decreed that medical units be self-sustaining, many local governments immediately sought foreign investment in for-profit, joint-venture health services. Foreign investors can often find excellent bargains in these kinds of opportunities. However, they may not be in the interest of the public or business community. In one case, one of the best local hospitals sought a joint-venture investment to develop a new cardiology unit catering to wealthy local merchants, senior government and Party cadres, and foreigners. However, if the scheme goes through, the hospital will transfer some of its best doctors and nurses to this unit and shut down a couple of low-cost public clinics. Is it ethical to invest in this profitable cardiology unit, knowing that it would deprive the poor of quality medical care? China also imports advanced medical equipment to perform forced abortions on pregnant women who violate the government's birth-control policy. Is participation in this policy ethical?

Sometimes the government implements politically motivated policies that make no sense from an economic standpoint. One of the northwestern provinces tried to attract Taiwanese investment. Political leaders believed that the more Taiwanese businesses had a financial stake in China, the less political resistance there would be to unite with China. The provincial government guaranteed the Taiwanese investors that it would buy energy for a premium price for a fixed period of time. Now the province already had a surplus of energy, yet the political leaders shut down several state-owned power plants, throwing thousands of people out of work.

Local political leaders commonly formulate discriminatory policies favoring foreign firms. Designated quotas of Foreign Direct Investment (FDI) often trigger resentment from local business communities. [7] Knowing that such a lucrative transaction might harm thousands of local workers, should one still go ahead? Should one invest in a deal knowing that it would be unfair to the local business community and trigger community tensions? These are tough questions for foreign investors, especially when the business environment is often shaped by top-down political policies. However, these policies may create a window of opportunity for foreign investors to enter the Chinese market. Therefore, to understand the market in China, wise business people need to closely monitor not only the economic indices but also the political dynamic.

State Owned Enterprises (SOEs)

Before 1979, all production and distribution were state-owned and organized under central planning. There was no private enterprise; there was no market. The main objective of these state owned enterprises (SOEs) was to meet the government's production quotas. Profit and loss were not considerations, because the cost, however high, would be absorbed by the state. Similarly, the state purchased all the goods and distributed these goods to various parties. As long as the government tried to run a planned economy, these SOEs enjoyed total stability and security.

An average SOE manager didn't care about economic gain or loss. That was not his or her responsibility. The manager's main duty was to oversee production to meet the assigned quota—often with no regard to the quality of the product. Frequently, however, production would idle for lack of raw materials. This was not the manager's fault, and the whole factory would simply suspend production. Workers would still get the same pay and benefits. An economic domino effect might suspend the operations of a whole series of factories in a vast chain of related SOEs. However, SOEs without money could just get fresh loans from the banks (also owned by the state). These loans would then be counted as credits, not liabilities. Banks that could not collect payments from other SOEs would just write them off. Unsold stock (such as obsolete items in the warehouse) would count as assets.

Each SOE was not only a production enterprise, but also a self-contained social unit designed by the state. Each SOE would provide everything from housing, medical care, and pensions to education and matchmaking for its employees and their dependents. Retired employees drew their benefits from the SOE until they died. Their privileges, such as housing and position, could then go to their descendants. Managers did not have the authority to hire and fire their staff. Only the government did, and all staff were expected to work until retirement. The government might assign new staff to an SOE, and the SOE manager would have to create jobs, regardless of the need, for them. That is because there is to be no unemployment in socialist China. It is common to see three or four people splitting a job that could be handled by one. Not surprisingly, a corporate culture of idling, slow work, redundancy, short hours, and low productivity is the norm.

Reforming these ailing SOEs, which still account for about half of China's Gross National Product (decreasing from almost 100 percent 20 years ago), is a tough challenge. On the one hand, the government can no longer afford to subsidize these inefficient enterprises in the face of intense competition from the private sector and joint venture enterprises that produce at lower cost and higher quality. On the other hand, the government cannot just write off these SOEs.

A large influx of unemployed and retired workers without pensions or social welfare support would create social instability. In general, the local government has few resources for social welfare, especially in economically depressed regions with an unusually high number of SOEs. The local government's meager resources cater mostly to orphans, lonely seniors, and disaster victims. They are nowhere near sufficient to handle massive numbers of unemployed workers. Only in recent years has the government begun to experiment with unemployment insurance, but only in a few cities such as Shanghai or Guangzhou, where there is concentrated wealth from the private sector. There are few safety nets for most SOE workers.

One of the most common SOE reform methods is to sell the business to investors or provide lucrative terms for joint ventures with foreigners. Hundreds of these SOEs can be acquired for almost nothing, but smart investors know there are many hidden costs.

One foreign investor purchased a state-owned drug company in the northeast for a fraction of the cost of a similar plant in another country. This SOE, with several subsidiaries, had been the sole supplier of drugs to government-run hospitals in the province. The foreign owner attempted to cut 30 percent of the employees. The workforce was three times larger than at comparable enterprises in the United States. If he could achieve that kind of a reduction, this company in theory could turn a profit within a year. However, he did not count on strong resistance both from the staff and the local government. Fully 25 percent of the town worked for this company. Another 10 percent were living on company pensions. Furthermore, most of the pensioners' housing depended on their children remaining company employees. Although the new owner legally could downsize this SOE and stop paying many pensioners, the harsh community reaction stopped him.

The final straw came when Beijing instituted a nationwide open-bid system for materials for all government hospitals, removing the SOE's monopoly. The new owner realized that the company could not compete with the price and quality of out-of-province suppliers. In addition, the local government would no longer provide subsidies to the company, because it was now a joint venture. In the end, he had to write off his investment, which ended up costing him several million dollars.

To forestall riots, the local government has had to inject capital into the company just to pay retired and current employees a minimum living allowance. The plant itself sits idle, and the government is in the red, surviving from handouts from the provincial government. SOE-related riots occasionally get reported. Some 400 workers from an obsolete copper mill in Shanxi were not paid for five years. A corrupt manager had pocketed the cash instead. [8]

Reforming SOEs is at the top of the government's agenda. It will be difficult, however. The government is constrained by its socialist ideology and a limited grasp of capitalism. Making these moribund enterprises and their dependent communities viable is a great challenge for foreigners. It is a high-risk opportunity, of course, but the rewards far eclipse any financial gains. Anyone who can revitalize these SOEs will be the guest of honor among senior government officials. Revitalized state owned enterprises certainly will become models for others. Successful entrepreneurs will have a large audience and tremendous influence on the cultural values in China. The government is desperately open to virtually any idea. It may even be open to formerly taboo areas such as religion. Can Christian business values revitalize dying communities? If so, they can be shared throughout China beyond the Chinese churches and into the hearts of tens of thousands of business people and government officials. These people otherwise have no such access to the Christian message.

Economic Polarization

During the first 30 years of socialism, the government artificially standardized all prices and incomes in China, regardless of the regional variations. The price of a bar of soap was basically the same whether you lived in Shanghai or Qinghai, even though the actual costs would vary from region to region. The government subsidized places where economic development was low and levied heavy taxes where it was high. In this way, economic inequality among citizens was limited. China could claim that everyone got more or less the same pay and benefits.

Still, China, a vast country, has a variety of regional differences. Each region has its own geographical and economic characteristics. The level of economic development varies greatly among them. They are the *southern coastal, eastern coastal, northeastern, northwestern, southwestern,* and *central regions.*

When China first began its economic reform plan by decreasing subsidies and increasing regional autonomy, the central government allowed regional governments to reinvest any profits within their regions. The *southern* and *eastern coastal* regions took off first. Very soon, an economic cycle appeared. The poor got poorer and the rich got richer. For the past 20 years, these regions have grown the fastest, in part because they benefit from excellent port transportation infrastructures, highly educated skilled labor, and a large influx of foreign investment. They boast familiar cities, such as Shanghai, Shenzhen, Guangzhou, Nanjing, Dalian, Hangzhou, and Xiamen. Most reports on China's economic reform come from these places. They present a general impression of economic boom times, prosperity, and liberalization. The images of these cities—with skyscrapers, construction cranes, superhighways, mobile phones, the Internet, and McDonald's—have become the icons of China's reform and prosperity.

The *northeastern region* is dominated by SOE heavy industries, such as steel and automobile manufacturing. It is a vast area with low population density, good infrastructure, rich mineral deposits, and fertile lands. This region had its heyday during the planned economy era. However, during the economic reform period, many of these largely subsidized

SOEs lacked the flexibility and technology to enter the market economy. Their products are obsolete. Today, many workers receive only meager living allowances and have to scramble to make ends meet. Some have gone to more prosperous provinces seeking jobs.

The *northwestern areas* are mainly arid lands with inefficient transportation networks. Many people here live below the absolute poverty line. [9] The *southwestern region*, meanwhile, is mostly mountainous with low-quality farmlands carved out from the hills. Most of the people are peasants; many of them live under the poverty line.

The *central region* consists of farmland. Its income depends heavily on the climate. Farmers can make good money with bumper crops—or face a total loss if there are floods.

The northeastern, northwestern, and central regions are home to over half of China's population and occupy 60 percent of the land. Yet they account for less than a quarter of the total Gross National Product. As the southern and eastern regions continue to develop, the economic gap between the regions simply widens. It is not uncommon to see some eastern Chinese enjoy annual incomes five to 10 times higher than their northwestern counterparts. A World Bank report found that the average annual income for a Shanghai resident in 1998 was around $3,500. It was just $420 for a Gansu resident in the northwest. [10]

Besides these geographical differences, there are also regional wage differences for similar professions. A manager in Shanghai can easily earn RMB 5,000 ($600) per month. In Xian, his counterpart would get RMB 800. A farmer in Jiangsu, in the eastern region, can earn RMB 20,000 to 30,000 per year. In Ningxia, in the northwestern region, a counterpart averages only RMB 1,000. A skilled worker can easily make RMB 2,000 per month in a Shenzhen factory. Workers in an average SOE in northeastern China, however, make RMB 100 to 150 per month. Many SOE employees often get nothing. There is also a general income gap between rural and urban people frequently in the magnitude of three to 10 times, depending on the region.

Therefore, there is really no average figure for income, wages, cost of living, and business expenses. China is an economically diverse country. The average Gross Domestic Product per capita is about $1,000, a rather low figure by international standards. However, Beijing ranks as the fourth most expensive city in the world to live. Shanghai is sixth. New York, for its part, ranks eighth, immediately followed by Guangzhou.[11] At the same time, China has more than 250 million people living on a dollar a day. One can hardly find any similarity between Shanghai, an international, cosmopolitan city on the eastern coast where mobile phones and the Internet are daily necessities, and Mujiang, a remote township inhabited by the Bulan minority in the southwest. There the government still uses hand-crank phones and runners to communicate with the various villages. The only common denominator between is that both places are under the same Chinese government. There is a whole spectrum of business practices in China, ranging from a barter system to e-commerce, and a whole range of production capacity from total manual labor of handicrafts to high-tech silicon chips and designer genetic drugs.

Anything is possible in China. It is no longer a nation where people wear blue and gray Mao jackets and ride on bicycles. Far from being a monolithic society, China is perhaps one of the most diverse countries in the world— geographically, ethnically, economically, and culturally. As the nation heads toward globalization, it will become even more diverse, as different regions develop at their own rates. Some will become more prosperous, others less.

It is, indeed, a great moral challenge for entrepreneurs to launch businesses that can both make money and lessen the economic tensions between rich and poor. The Bible speaks many ways about God's concern for the poor. Christian business people also need to care. They can do so, in part, by considering business opportunities for the disadvantaged in poor regions. While business options for the poor may not make much sense from a financial perspective, they are a moral approach that is essential to bringing harmony to China's increasingly economically polarized nation. Can Christian business practices become viable alternative models in China to provide both profits and a more just allocation of resources? Or does the Christian entrepreneurial spirit only benefit the haves and put the have-nots in a disadvantaged position? This is the critique the communists have always leveled against the capitalists. May God help us prove their analysis wrong.

Population Migration

When economic liberalization began over two decades ago, officials saw fit to organize economic centers that require large amounts of labor. For example, in the 1980s, the Pearl River Delta region in southern Guangdong started one of the first special economic zones (SEZs). The goal was to attract foreign investment for labor-intensive manufacturing. Many semi-skilled laborers from interior provinces sought employment in that region. The payment was several times more than working in the farm. Soon the SEZ city of Shenzhen was built from a small village. It drew economic migrants from all over China. Currently 7 million people live in Shenzhen. Several million more migrant laborers work in the surrounding region in tens of thousands of factories. Similar economic regions also have emerged in regions. They attract millions of migrant laborers, construction and factory workers, and those willing to do manual tasks that the locals in major cosmopolitan centers do not. There are from 80 million to perhaps 120 million internal migrants in China. This huge population has begun to have a huge impact on China.

Economic polarization is the main force behind this migration movement. Traditionally, people have flowed from the poor interior provinces to the more prosperous coastal provinces. This was the major trend in the 1980s and the early 1990s, when most of the economic growth took place along the coastal areas. However, as the urban centers required more services and goods, there has been a new mass movement in China. People now congregate in mega-metropolises (such as Shanghai, Beijing, and Chongqing, with more than 10 million people in each place). They are establishing new cities from former townships and villages. This urbanization process, induced by economic reform, brings about new social dynamics, with profound business and missiological implications.

First of all, the massive movement of population began to undermine the long established Residential Registration Policy, which categorized people as belonging either to rural or urban population groups. This policy also restricted people's movements. In the past, an SOE could not draw workers from outside its own area. Out-of-towners who wanted a job had to apply for temporary residential permits. They also had to transfer residency to the new area. Overcoming these rules was costly and troublesome. With the economic boom, which triggered massive migration of laborers to these new areas, officials simply could not keep up with residential registration anymore. The government is being forced to abolish its long-standing residential policy. This may bring about revolutionary social changes in China. Rural populations are no longer bound to villages with little economic future People can choose to live where they can make a living. The Ningpao municipality in Zhejiang recently abolished its own policy, and other areas will soon follow suit. In effect, people can now travel freely and live anywhere they wish as long as they can afford it. This sea change in employment also allows businesses to openly recruit talent from across the nation. Obtaining a residential permit is no longer an issue. These developments, not incidentally, will also help Christian workers travel freely throughout China.

This migration also allows people to bring business opportunities to remote places. The economic boom has fueled the massive movement of people to the remotest frontiers of China. Merchants apparently will have virtually open access to every region and people group in China. Many of these migrants are small business people who would go anywhere for a business opportunity.

The Wenzhou merchants, who have a long tradition of aggressive and successful trading, are a prime example. When China's market began to liberalize, the Wenzhou people were the first to manufacture all kinds of household goods. They catered to peasants, who hitherto had little disposable income. The Wenzhou merchants are the pioneers of the liberal market economy in China. Currently, 98 percent of the province's GDP comes from private enterprise, which is the highest rate in the nation. Wenzhou established the country's first guild-style organization—the Wenzhou Lighter Industrial Association—to protect their intellectual rights to the goods they design. [12] The Wenzhou merchants also set up their own nationwide distribution network. Traveling to remote areas, they were often the first group to pioneer markets. Soon, many others followed them into the developing economic markets in virtually every corner of China.

One can hardly underestimate the power of such a movement if harnessed for the kingdom. Many Wenzhou merchants indeed are kingdom-minded Christians. Wenzhou boasts the highest percentage of Christians in any urban center in China (15 percent according to official statistics, and up to 30 percent by other estimates). That means there are 1-2 million extremely evangelism-minded Christians out of the population of 7 million in Wenzhou. Wherever these Christian merchants go, they establish Christian meetings and hold services. For pragmatic economic reasons, local officials usually turn a blind eye. These merchants are nearly everywhere, from the Sino-Russian border near Siberia to the Sino-Burmese border, from the Tibetan plateau in Qinghai to the Kulun Mountain next to Afghanistan. Currently Christian merchants from Wenzhou have organized the only sanctioned Christian meeting points in Lhasa, Tibet. They are receiving favor from Tibetans, one of the most difficult peoples in the world to reach. With more mission-minded merchants and entrepreneurs in China, the missiological implications would be enormous, particularly among unreached groups.

✳ A final point in population migration involves reaching the people who have taken temporary jobs in urban factories before returning to their home villages with money in their pockets. When they return home, they usually also bring back new skills and ideas. Many local churches around such factories are reaching out to them, and the response has been impressive.

For example, the church in Boan near Shenzhen was once a small preaching point of the Basel Mission, when the town was nothing more than a small farming village before 1949. The church opened again in the 1980s with two dozen old folks. However, the government designated Boan as a special economic zone, and within 10 years the population grew from tens of thousands to a few million. Most of these newcomers were short-term factory workers. These workers often suffer from homesickness and loneliness.

With minimal recreational facilities available, some turned to the local church out of curiosity. Soon many of them became Christians. Seizing the opportunity, church elders initiated a series of evangelistic campaigns, often in coordination with Christian merchants from Hong Kong who own factories in Boan. It is quite common to spot evangelists and pastors from Hong Kong who are hired as "personnel managers." Soon the Boan Church grew to several thousand in attendance. The church holds three worship services each Sunday in a new seven-story building. Its pastoral training center is open all year. Many converts receive pastoral training while working in Boan. When they return home, they are often the first Christians in their villages. The Boan Church has members from every province in China, and most will return to their homes as Christian witnesses.

The Boan Church is truly a missionary-sending church that takes advantage of the dynamics of economic migration. This ministry is possible because of the support of Christian business people who invest in Boan and are willing live out the Great Commission. They sacrificially provide not only employment but also Christian love to economic migrants. As these migrants return to their homes, they will carry with them seeds sown during their brief encounter with a Christian enterprise. No one can predict how these seeds may germinate: 30-, 50-, or 100-fold. Only God knows where these seeds may take root, but they may be in places beyond our imagination.

Chapter 4

The WTO Accession

The first modern encounter between China and the West centered on international trade. It was not a happy encounter. As we saw earlier, China exported silk and tea to Europe in the early 19th century, leading to a large trade surplus for China. Meanwhile, European merchants had a hard time entering China's domestic market due to the isolation policy of the Qing Dynasty. Later, the British developed China's opium market to such an extent that the trade balance was reversed, even to the point of bankrupting the Qing government. The Opium War was a consequence of this trade war.

The following century saw no effective governance in China. The economy was at the mercy of the powerful West. Not without some justification, China interpreted this period as semi-colonialism. Western nations were taking advantage of China through trade. Foreign goods flooded the Chinese markets, and local craftsmen had a hard time competing with these mass-produced, high quality goods. With its adoption of socialism in 1949, China effectively cut itself off from the economic activities of the West, where economic growth had been accelerating through free enterprise and trade.

Finally, in the early 1980s, China again began to open to the West. Since the early 1990s, China has been determined to link with the rest of the world economically. China's entrance into the World Trade Organization (WTO) symbolizes its coming of age in the international economy. It also marks the second major economic encounter between China and the rest of the world. However, this time China is not being forced to trade with the West. Instead, it is actively asserting its economic strength in the international community. This new posture bears far-reaching sociopolitical and economic implications that will lead China to the point of no return socially. China will intimately link with the rest of the world through business and trade. There are some issues related to the WTO that have a significant bearing on the missionary enterprise.

Opportunities and Risks

When one nation trades with another, each side wants to forge a trade surplus, and for obvious reasons. To produce wealth, each wants to sell more than it buys. Many nations set up trade barriers to discourage imports or foreign involvement in domestic markets. The common signs of trade protectionism are high import taxes, laws restricting foreigners from entering domestic markets, import quotas, preferential treatment for local products and industries, and restrictive regulations on imported items. The most common way for a nation to boost exports is to subsidize their production so that they may be sold at a low price in the world market. However, such trade barriers and subsidies are not free trade, which we can define as fair and open competition. Further, they may spark a trade war. The most effective markets allow fair competition, which generates the most efficient production and the highest quality of products for smaller price tags. Taken together, these factors produce wealth.

It is difficult for any country both to protect its own industry from import competition while encouraging the export of its goods to other nations. Those nations with a weak manufacturing base—usually the developing countries—are at a competitive disadvantage with more developed countries. However, these relatively poor countries can compensate somewhat because they pay lower wages. They can produce cheaper low-end products, and their exports can threaten jobs and production in more developed and expensive nations. This results in a redistribution of production and jobs worldwide. Usually, however, economically weak countries are at the mercy of economically strong nations and multinational corporations (MNCs).

Following World War II, in the late 1940s, the international community established the General Agreement on Tariffs and Trade (GATT) to ensure fair and open competition in international trade. GATT sought to promote low tariffs and to balance the business interests of different nations. China was one of its founding members but later was represented by the U.S.-backed regime in Taiwan for political reasons. GATT has been, for a long time, dominated by Western economic powers. In 1995 GATT became the World Trade Organization to reflect the changing dynamics and increasing complexity of international political and economic reality. The WTO aims to address issues such as multilateral trades, economic globalization, various new international trade practices of MNCs, and the emergence of the Asian economic powers. China has applied for membership since 1986. What followed were more than 15 years of marathon talks over issues such as human rights and intellectual property. The final session concluded on September 18, 2001, when China was approved to enter the WTO.

WTO member countries agree to abide by mutual trade principles, standards, and regulations. Under threat of sanction by other members of the WTO, participating nations agree to keep tariffs low and access high for foreign businesses in their domestic markets. Governments also pledge to maintain transparency in business decisions, to produce clear and effective legislation on trade and commercial activities, to diminish any import quotas, and to remove subsidies on exports. The aim of these measures is to create an international market. There is supposed to be only one integrated market of all the member nations. Any nation that joins the WTO must open its market to all other nations. In return, it has access to their markets. The decision to enter the WTO, of course, carries tremendous opportunities as well as risks.

As China concluded its negotiations in Geneva, it announced that foreign investors no longer would need to partner with national enterprises. It removed restrictions on foreign remittance, and abolished export quotas on goods produced in China by foreign-owned firms. [13] In other words, China no longer requires foreign firms to team up with Chinese partners to run businesses. A foreign firm can establish a wholly owned company, together with branch offices and subsidiaries. Further, there is no restriction on the amount of profit companies can send out of the country. In the past, there was a limit on foreign currency that a company could take out of China as profit. Finally, the removal of export quotas means that a foreign company can manufacture and sell all its products in China without the need to export a certain percentage.

China has also pledged to open up its financial, insurance, telecommunication, and transportation sectors to foreign enterprises. However, it will not open the military industry, the state-controlled media, and some traditional arts and crafts to foreigners. In sum, these measures suggest that China is opening its domestic market, and foreign firms can have a wider degree of freedom to conduct their businesses.

China's WTO entry is an opportunity for foreign business people to reach 1.3 billion consumers—the largest single market in the world. The sky really might be the limit. China is even talking about opening its growing domestic airlines to foreign involvement, a field that hitherto had been jealously guarded by two dozen state-owned airlines. Code-sharing schemes are already in effect between China Eastern and Delta, both in China and in the United States. Similar arrangements between other partners are in the works as well. [14] International firms in insurance, finance, banking, entertainment, and travel see China as the next important market to capture.

The opening of China's market is especially significant

in light of the current global economic slowdown. While the economies of the United States, the European Union, and Japan are struggling, a problem made worse by the September 11, 2001, terrorist attacks, China is the only major economic power still managing to achieve steady economic growth. In fact, the terrorist attacks actually ended up boosting many China stocks, as the country has been seen as a relatively safe haven. It is not involved in the current conflict between Islamic extremists and the Western powers. China's huge internal market is an insatiable giant that consumes all kinds of local and imported goods. [15] On the supply side, China is now the largest producer of toys, clothing, footwear, and lighters and the third largest information technology manufacturer in the world.[16] China continues to draw the second largest amount of direct foreign investment in the world after the United States.

Many Chinese firms have special access to or dominance in markets in some countries for political and historical reasons: Laos, Myanmar, Iran, Iraq, Libya, Cuba, the five Central Asian republics, Siberia (Russia), North Korea, Syria, Yugoslavia, Zambia, Tanzania, and Mongolia. Chinese and foreign enterprises can forge new alliances to develop unique markets.

Chinese merchants also operate the two largest household commodity wholesale markets in Eastern Europe. One of them is the famous Four Tigers Market in Budapest, which supplies over half the clothing and footwear in the region. Strategic alliances with Chinese firms allow businesses to enter new markets even beyond the WTO areas. Not incidentally, these markets are in countries that have the strongest resistance to missionary activities as well as anti-Western sentiments. Yet they are open for merchants, especially merchants from China. A kingdom-minded merchant just cannot afford to overlook this opportunity.

Despite the sheer size and potential of the China market, there are many risks one cannot ignore. One of the most challenging is China's lack of a clear legal system, which the

West has enjoyed as a key component in its economic growth for centuries. In the past, the Chinese legal system—the public security office, the prosecution office, and the courts—has served only the interests and policies of the Party. It has been merely a tool of the Party to govern the nation. Since the 1980s, however, China has taken steps toward nationwide legal reform, from absolute rule by the Party to the rule of law. Beijing has passed a range of new laws, revamped the legal apparatus, and granted more rights to citizens. It has also passed new legislation to facilitate foreign business involvement in China.

Despite these reforms, however, there has been little political will to enforce them. Whenever a commercial dispute comes up, business people have little confidence in and respect for the judgment of the courts. Further, there has been virtually no enforcement of court decisions when rendered. Therefore, foreign investors often rely on non-legal means in commercial disputes, such as political intervention from their own country or powerful figures through *guanxi*.

The WTO accession forces China to strengthen its legal system. Thankfully, there are some encouraging signs. Authorities have passed the Arbitration Law, established an International Arbitration Tribunal, and introduced international law in Chinese courts for commercial cases. These measures and others will speed up legal protection for foreign investors. However, it will take a long time for these reforms, already unfolding in major cities such as Shanghai and Beijing, to be diffused into the lesser-developed regions, where foreign investment is most needed.

Differences According to Industry

China will face many new challenges when cheap imports flood its own market. At the same time, other sectors in China's economy will be able to take advantage of new markets overseas. China is not an economic monolith, and different economic sectors will experience different consequences. In general, light industry, intensive labor commodities—such as clothing and toys—will do well. China has already captured a significant portion of the world market for these goods. Cheaper imported raw materials, such as steel and sugar, will surely benefit these manufacturing industries. The IT sector is uncertain for the moment. It has shown an increasing ability to produce state-of-the-art products with help from Taiwan business people. [17] About 2,000 out-of-work executives from Silicon Valley flocked to Shanghai to compete for 234 senior jobs in China's IT industry at a recent job fair. [18] Many Chinese in this sector are enthused about the WTO accession and predict a huge expansion in this field.

However, many sectors in the economy may face a bleak outlook. The agricultural and auto sectors in particular face an uncertain future with respect to the WTO.

Agricultural Sector

China has to feed almost a fourth of the world's population but with only 7 percent of the world's arable land. This enormous disparity has heavily taxed the land. Most of the nutrients in the soil have been depleted. Farmers have continuously worked some lands, especially in the central and northwestern regions, for almost 2,000 years. In fact, only 40 percent of China's farmlands produce medium and high yields. The rest produce low yields. In order to produce sufficient food, these low-yield areas are home to about 70 percent of the population. These 900 million people cultivate almost all the available farmland, using labor-intensive methods. In a typical Chinese village, every available patch of land has some kind of crop planted on it.

China has been a net importer of grain, and the major global customer for wheat, for many years. With its agricultural technology generally low tech, its farms are small. Almost every peasant familys farms a plot of land of less than 2 acres per person. Compare this with the only other nation to have a billion people. India has more than twice the farmland per capita than China has. In fact, the production efficiency of China is extremely low—it only reaches 0.4 metric tons per capita annually. Developed nations' output ranges from 90 to 140 metric tons. Another point to remember is that most of the people in China are peasants. In developed nations, however, the poorest people usually comprise less than 20 percent. Further, China's peasants are less productive agriculturally than the poor of many other nations. Although there is an inexhaustible pool of cheap labor, the costs of major agricultural products in China are still about 30 percent higher than in the rest of the world because of low efficiency.

Without the customary high tariffs and agricultural subsidies they have benefited from for years, many farming sectors will collapse under the WTO. For example, due to a domestic surplus, the price of sugar in China (1999) was RMB 2,400 per metric ton, down from 3,200 in 1998. However, the world market price in 1999 was only RMB 1,700. If China had not imposed a high tariff, cheaper imported sugar could easily have destroyed China's sugar industry. The country's cotton, [19] edible oil, wheat, and dairy sectors are all facing a similar predicament.

Some agricultural sectors are producing at lower than the world price, including the poultry, pork, fishing, and fruit industries. In fact, China is the largest fruit and fishery producer in the world. However, the quality of its fruit is fairly low, so China can export it only to certain countries. China's inability to process and package its foods to world standards is another major challenge. Fish and meat exports require a high level of processing to meet high food hygiene standards. Otherwise, they can only be shipped to neighboring countries as perishable goods with low shelf lives and little add-on-value. This sector requires large investments of capital to upgrade its food-processing facilities if China is to compete in the world agricultural market.

With admittance into the WTO, China will have to lower its agricultural subsidy ceiling to 8.5 percent. As a result, many agricultural sectors will collapse. However, some sectors, including local food production, may benefit from cheaper imported raw materials. Cheaper sugar, butter, and flour surely will help China's baking industry become more competitive. To keep many peasant farmers from losing their livelihoods, the government will have to pour in large amounts of capital to improve farming techniques and enhance the quality of crops (such as higher quality cotton). If it doesn't, these out-of-work farmers will swell the ranks of landless peasants, already estimated at 100 million. They will become either a constant supply of cheap labor for other economic sectors or a social time bomb.

Auto Industry

In the past, China's auto industry was geared toward trucks and buses, not passenger cars. Production lines dated from Soviet times. The flagship of China's sedan production, Red Flag Auto Factory, was in fact a German assembly line looted by the Red Army after the Second World War and given to China in the early 1950s. China has four major state-owned car-making companies, but they produce mainly commercial vehicles. There are about 100 smaller SOEs, operated by local governments, which manufacture various types of sedans. Some of these sedans, however, are basically motorized buggies.

Most major international automakers have launched joint ventures in China in order to get a foothold in this untapped market. Many analysts have predicted that, with economic growth of 7-8 percent annually, soon China will have a large middle class that will be purchasing automobiles. Car sales in 1999 reached about 570,000 units and will probably hit 1 million by 2005. [20] The number could likely go higher if manufacturers can launch more low-price models. The WTO requires that China gradually lower the current 100 percent tariff to around 25 percent in the next five years. Needless to say, this will be a shock to the whole industry.

Major players, such as Volkswagen, Chrysler, and General Motors, are already imparting their production know-how in joint ventures with SOEs. They employ local staff. Despite the relatively low wages of Chinese workers, the product cost in China is rather high by international standards. For example, a medium sedan, such as the Volkswagen Santana, costs $7,000 to manufacture in the international market. Yet it costs $10,000 to produce in China, under the most optimal conditions. On average, it costs $12,000-$14,000 to produce such a vehicle in Shanghai, about twice the international price. The most modern auto manufacturing facility in China is the General Motors plant in Shanghai. There it costs this modern, hence most efficient, plant at least $35,000 to assemble a luxury Buick model. However, in Detroit it costs only $18,000 to make the same car. The current tariff still makes the local Buick a better buy. However, with the lowering of the tariff, the U.S.-made Buick will cost only $22,500 plus shipping. Who will buy a locally made U.S. car when the genuine article is about half the cost? Furthermore, there are tens of thousands of cheap Korean and Japanese cars waiting to flood the China market once the tariff is lowered.

Cars cost a lot to produce in China—despite low wages and some modern facilities—for three major reasons. One, every auto manufacturer in China is an SOE. That means they are inherently overstaffed and inefficient. Central government reform measures cannot do much to change things as long as local governments and ministries heavily protect these factories as the pillar industries of their respective districts. Even joint ventures face enormous managerial challenges. Foreign investors have virtually no power to discipline Chinese employees, who are SOE staff.

Two, there is too much manufacturing capacity. Nearly all automakers overestimated demand in China in the early and mid-1990s as they expanded their plants. They also underestimated the number of players who suddenly entered the sector. Thus, they are running at only one-third of capacity. Unlike other vehicle manufacturers, few operate in shifts. Because of their underutilized, depreciating assets and high overhead (many retain full administrative staff on payrolls), the automobiles they do produce cost a lot.

Three, most of the production lines are well behind the times technologically. Even for the newest plants, the technology used is already 10 years behind. Few foreign companies want to share their latest technologies with China, fearing that they will be stolen.

All this adds up to the fact that China's auto industry is facing serious WTO-related challenges. On the one hand, it takes no genius to predict that China's domestic auto market will boom with the rapid expansion of the middle class. On the other hand, reasonably priced, quality cars will flood the market as soon as the tariffs are dropped. The local and joint venture makers have a few advantages left, such as 25 percent tariff protection, knowledge of the local market and support, and immediate access to customers without expensive transportation costs. However, these manufacturers in China must transform their production efficiency within a few years or be ousted by imports. The government, of course, hopes that the WTO accession can put pressure on these inefficient manufacturers to shape up. No matter which outcome happens, there will be a large number of layoffs and possibly a large number of new jobs created by new joint ventures or foreign or privately owned enterprises entering China's automobile markets. There will be new mergers or forms of joint venture taking place in this sector.[21] In addition, there will also be a growing industry of spin-off–parts, services, and accessories.

The Go-West Campaign

As we have seen, different economic sectors in China will be affected differently. These sectors also coincide with regions and widen the nation's regional economic polarization. Most of the heavy industries and SOEs are in the northeast. This region will suffer massive layoffs. Although there may be new investment into these industries, these laid-off workers may not qualify for the newly created jobs. But these new jobs may also bring in fresh money that will trickle down to the poorer societal sectors. There are still many natural resources in the northeastern region, such as forests, and many surplus laborers may turn to other economic sectors.

At the same time, the eastern and southern regions may accelerate their economic growth, since most of the nation's export-oriented light industries and IT enterprises are concentrated there. Also, most of the high yield farmlands are in these regions. Therefore, the WTO entry will help these regions experience a major economic boom. Living standards will rise, and all kinds of services will increase. This boom will attract talented people from the lesser-developed areas, further fueling rapid economic development.

The southwestern and northwestern regions are currently the poorest areas in China. Per capita Gross Domestic Product (GDP) is one-half to one-third of the other regions. Most likely the rich economic centers in the south and east will continue to draw talent and wealth from the western regions, further slowing their development. The WTO will accelerate this process of economic disparity and create huge social tensions, possibly even social unrest. These two western regions already face social tensions because of existing ethnic and religious conflicts. Quite a high percentage of the inhabitants are from minority groups, such as the Hui (Muslim), the Urgyur, the Tibetan, the Jingpo (Kuchin), and the Va. These tensions may easily cause regional instability. It is a scenario few would like to see.

In order to fairly balance the rate of economic development in the different regions vis-à-vis the WTO accession, the government initiated an ambitious 10-year, RMB 1,000 billion project in 2000 called the Go-West Campaign. It is a sort of Marshall Plan to build a communication, transportation, irrigation, and energy infrastructure to boost economic development in these high altitude plateaus, deserts, and mountains. The government hopes that this infrastructure will enhance the competitiveness of these underdeveloped regions and attract investors. It will also encourage the skilled laborers and technicians in these regions to stay instead of looking for opportunities elsewhere. The government has passed regional tax breaks and incentive packages for foreign investors. There are special offices, publications, and exposure trips for investors. [22]

Developing the western part of China is indeed a challenge. It has more than half of China's land and about a third of the population. It produces less than a fifth of the nation's GDP, is populated with most of China's poorest people, has at least 40 national minority groups, and has the harshest living environment in China. However, it strategically has access to two important regions: Central Asia and Southeast Asia. The northwestern region is the crossroads between China and Europe, famous for the historic Silk Road. It is close to Afghanistan, Tajikistan, Kazakhstan, Kyrgyzstan, Pakistan, and India. Through these nations, China can have access to Europe. One of the Go-West projects is to build several commercial hubs between Asia and Europe. Soon, goods between China and Europe can go through these new Silk Roads. Another project is to link gas and oil pipelines with the Middle East and Central Asia.

Another ambitious Go-West project is to develop the whole Mekong River region (China, Laos, Myanmar, Vietnam, Thailand, and Cambodia) as an integrated economic zone. China has already expanded border-trading facilities with Myanmar, Laos, and Vietnam to accelerate the rapid growth of cross-border trading. Chinese business people also invest heavily in this region and are hoping to develop the Mekong River (originating in China and crossing the above-mentioned nations) as the Rhine River of Southeast Asia. A new railway to link China with Myanmar and going all the way to Singapore is under construction. Soon China's southwest may become a major influencer of several Southeast Asian countries. [23]

The Go-West Campaign is a government-initiated economic development project to bring a more equal distribution of resources with China's entry into the WTO. It is an administrative means to help people with lesser resources in a highly competitive society. From a socialist perspective, it is a mandate to help the proletarians and to protect the poor from the exploitation of capitalists. Otherwise, the rich will get richer and the poor poorer in a globalized market economy.

Christians, too, embrace such a notion of sharing resources with the poor, knowing that such giving may not have ideal returns, at least in a monetary sense. For Christian entrepreneurs, it is an opportunity to express biblical values by channeling investments into these areas, fully aware that the return may not be as high as in the eastern or southern regions. However, such investments may help bring about a more just society.

Not to be overlooked is the fact that a high percentage of the popuce have had minimal contact with or understanding of Christianity. Christian entrepreneurs can witness to these people through their economic involvement. Further, economic activities in these two regions usually spread into many other nations—nations that have little access to the gospel themselves. They are 10/40 Window mission frontiers that have been mostly closed to traditional missionaries and mission activities. From a missiological perspective, we cannot overlook their close economic ties with China.

The Future of China

The WTO accession draws diverse predictions—from paradise to doomsday. Gordon G. Chang's controversial *The Coming Collapse of China* suggests that China will face dire consequences as it opens its door for cheap imports. [24] He predicts that increasing unrest among the laid-off workers, compounded by the corruption among the bureaucrats, will bring social chaos to China. The other major WTO concern is China's farming community. The nation has to brace for the probable collapse of many farms when cheaper agricultural products pour in. In fact, there is already much unrest among peasants due to high taxes.[25] Chinese peasants in many places are already living a marginal existence. They got the worst deal during the "Open and Reform" period and now have to face another blow from the WTO. If hungry and desperate peasants begin to flood the cities, China could be ignited.[26] Finally, there is the hidden time bomb of China's unhealthy banks. Non-performing loans are as high as an alarming 50 percent among the four state-owned banks. These loans are mostly non-recoverable.[27] Laid-off workers, corruption, bankrupt farmers, and failing state-banks all contribute to a rather gloomy picture.

On the other hand, many Chinese citizens will be economically blessed by the WTO. For example, the IT field expects a quantum leap in the global market. The light industry sector expects more foreign investment and an increase in exports. Many figures support such an assumption. The average Chinese wage is $780 per year, much lower than Malaysia's $3,390 or South Korea's $8,490. Hence China may attract more investors seeking to take advantage of its lower wage scales.[28] Further, China is the only major country that has experienced no significant economic setback related to September 11. In fact, a lot of capital has poured in. China seems to be a safe haven in this conflict. Many analysts predict that entry in the WTO will sustain China's amazing 7-8 percent annual economic growth rate.

For the society as a whole, the WTO accession will accelerate the current trend of social plurality. Citizens will have more options in jobs, living, travel, and entertainment. China will have to speed up its legal reform from the current "Rule by Law" to an eventual "Rule of Law." Thus, people will receive more legal rights. Eventually, this trend will challenge the Party's monopoly on power. It may even fundamentally transform the sociopolitical system. There are signs that the government is heading in this direction.[29] It is gradually abolishing the citizen registry system so that people can choose where they live so long as they can afford it. However, such plurality and diversity will create new classes of rich and poor people, in both urban and rural areas. Such a social phenomenon is part and parcel of economic development. The government is attempting to address it, through means such as the Go-West Campaign.

On the religious front, there may be increasing numbers of new believers, as religious awakening often accompanies social change. The government may relax its tight religious controls against currently unregistered (and technically illegal) religious groups to create a buffer against the social shock from the WTO entry. Further, seeing a possible influx of people who need help, the government will allow more social services to be provided by nongovernmental organizations, including religious groups, to supplement its own meager social services. For pragmatic reasons, the government will tolerate religion, even religious growth, as long as religious groups can help sustain a stable and prosperous society. The government seems to particularly welcome foreign business people, religious or otherwise, as long as they can bring prosperity to China.

The WTO accession takes China on a new, uncharted course that will perhaps change it forever. By inviting entrepreneurs into the Party, an anathema to communist ideology, the Chinese Communist Party is giving the nod to pragmatism over ideology. Such change is inevitable, as China becomes part of the economic globalization process. This process will also create an ideological vacuum, temporarily filled by secularism and materialism. However, as people begin to search more for transcendent values, especially in an increasingly economically polarized society, it will be a golden opportunity for Christians to provide an answer relevant both in the luxury shopping malls and in the poor rural farms.

China is genuinely open to practical ideas. Whoever can provide them may lead China onto higher moral and spiritual ground.

Notes

1 *China Statistic Annual*, 1999.

2 "China has largest trade gap with US," *South China Morning Post*, 22 February 2001.

3 In one of the official Qing court documents, we read that Europeans needed tea from China because they would get sick if they did not have tea in their diet to help the digestion of cheese, which they ate in large quantities. Therefore, as a show of mercy to those "barbaric" foreigners, the emperor allowed China to sell them tea. This incident shows the lack of international knowledge among the court officials and the rationale behind these trade decisions. Further, there seems to be a lack of common sense as well: How did these European "barbarians" survive before they heard of tea from China? With such a "strategic" commodity at hand, why didn't China threaten to bring the Europeans to their knees?

4 There were 13 trading houses established in Guangzhou to deal with all foreign merchants. These houses could set the price, levy the tax, and act as a go-between for foreigners and the Chinese government. One can hardly define it as purely private or purely governmental. In fact, the nature of these trading houses is both civil and governmental.

5 During the late 19th century, the Chinese government attempted to catch up with the West, especially in military weapons. It bought many factories to produce weapons. It also opened shipyards to build warships. It sent many people abroad to learn Western technology. Its slogans were: "Using the Western technology as tools, but Chinese tradition as the governing system" and "Using the foreign tools to fight the foreigners." The leaders were not aware of the fact that technology is always in progress. Often China spent much money to purchase outdated or obsolete equipment. Further, they failed to see that Western technological development could not be separated from Western social development, such as individualism and democracy, which provided a social basis for creative development.

6 The absolute poverty standard established by the Chinese government is RMB 500-800 per year ($65-80 per year). This cannot feed an individual. There are still 50-60 million people living below this line. The United Nations' standard is $1 per day. If we use the U.N. standard, the figure will

be 100-200 million people living below the internationally recognized line of absolute poverty.

7   *China Economic Journal,* August 3, 2001. http://finance.sina.com.cn/d/ 20010803/91102.html

8   See Xinhuanet news at http://news.sina.com.cn/c/2001-08-03/ 319827.html. August 3, 2001.

9   China's absolute poverty line is about one quarter of the U.N. standard of $1 per capita per day.

10 "China: Politic and Power," *Stratfor Strategic Forecasting,* May 17, 2001, in www.stratfor.com/asia/cointries/china/politic3.htm.

11 "Counting the Cost of Living in Asia," *Far East Economic Review,* August 17, 2001, p. 12.

12 David Murphy, "Charge of Lighter Brigade," in *Far East Economic Review,* August 23, 2001, pp. 46-47.

13 See the news bulletin by the Chinese government, September18, 2001, http://news.sina.com.cn/c/2001-09-18/360762.html.

14 China just signed a $1.6 billion deal to purchase 30 Boeing 737s. Boeing forecasts China will need 1,764 new commercial jets over the next 20 years, the largest jetliner market outside of the United States. See Associated Press: "China, Boeing ink $1.6 billion deal" (October 2, 2001) at http://www.msnbc.com/news/ 637055.asp.

15 See the analysis on the post-September 11 event on China's economy, October 8, 2001, at http://finance.sina.com.cn /g/ 20011008/ 113927.html.

16 China will probably overtake Japan, which ranks second in IT products, by 2002, *Asiaweek,* July 27-August 3, 2001, p. 36.

17 See Jim Erickson's "The Next Super Power" in *Asiaweek* (July 27–3 August, 2001), pp. 34-42, a special feature report on China's IT industry.

18 See *Asiaweek* (August 17, 2001), p. 8.

19 For example, see the extensive report on the cotton industry in China in *Business & Finance Review* [*Caijing Magazine*], No. 44, September, 2001, pp. 22-38.

20 Special Issue on China, *Asiaweek* (March 30-April 6, 2001), pp. 64-65.

21 *China Northern Journal* (July 29, 2001), p. 12.

22 For example, the magazine *West China* publishes articles on various investment opportunities as well as local regulations favoring investors.

23 See Yang Hongchang, *Co-operation Between Yunnan Province and Mekong River Region: The Development of Regional Autonomy in China* (Hong Kong: Asia-Pacific Research Institute of the Chinese University of Hong Kong, 2001).

24 See Gordon G. Chang's "The Shah of Beijing" in *Far East Economic Review* (September 13, 2001), p. 31.

25 See Frank Langfitt's "Chinese peasants slain amid tax dispute," in *Baltimore Sun* (April 22, 2001).

26 An excellent source of studies in this field is Jean Hung, editor, *Coming into Chinese Country in the Twenty First Century* (Beijing: Guangming Press, 2000).

27 See David Lague, "Life at the Edge of Chaos," in *Far East Economic Review* (October 4, 2001), pp. 70-71.

28 "China: Poised for Major Growth," in *Stratfor Strategic Forecasting* (September 10, 2001), http://stratfor.com/asia/commentary/0109101530.html.

29 Stanley Lubman, "Trying Times: WTO Entry Will Challenge China's Legal System" in *Asiaweek* (March 30-April 6, 2001), p. 38.

PART TWO:

Models

Since 1980, the Chinese Christian church has reemerged from the ruins of persecution and grown into an astonishing community numbering in the millions. Its members come from all walks of life, including business. In the context of socialist China, it is indeed a challenge for Chinese Christian entrepreneurs to run for-profit businesses while maintaining high Christian ethical standards. However, some Chinese Christian entrepreneurs have already developed models that combine successful business practices and Christian witness beyond the government-confined church activities. These Chinese business leaders are creating new paradigms for holistic entrepreneurs in regions where Christianity is restricted. Some of the models and their examples are given here. These case studies were conducted during 2001.

Chapter 5

Christian Witnessing Model

Because religious activities are restricted to government-designated venues, projecting Christian influence beyond the four walls of the church building is difficult. However, many Christians choose to bring their values and faith into their business practices. As their influence spreads, they become a beacon of truth to their colleagues. Beyond this, their ethical practices even influence the industries in which they work.

Case Study: The Interior Decoration Tycoon of Shanghai, Jiang Jiexue, and Shanghai Qianxi Ltd.

The Call

Mr. Jiang Jiexue's mother is a very devoted Christian from Suzhou near Shanghai. Mrs. Jiang introduced the faith to her son while he was very young. He had attended Christian meetings since he was a child, and he still reads the Bible and prays every morning. After he finished his schooling, Mr. Jiang went to Shanghai to seek employment. Now both Mrs. Jiang and her son attend the Shanghai International Church.

Mr. Jiang first worked at Shanghai's Public Security Bureau (PSB) as an officer for 12 years. During his tenure, he suggested many innovative ideas and was able to streamline the resolution process of some cases. However, Jiang did not feel satisfied or fulfilled. He felt that the bureaucratic system was stifling his creativity. He felt that God had given him gifts in innovation and creativity, and that he should fully develop this potential in life. In 1988, he left the PSB and launched his own business.

The Entrepreneurial Launch

Jiang had taught himself interior design by reading books and by observation. In the late 1980s, Shanghai had begun to experience economic prosperity, and many of its citizens spent money on home improvements. In general, people still lived in tiny flats so storage space was at a premium. Jiang ingeniously designed hidden closets so that they did not obstruct the sense of space. He also pioneered a modular furniture system that was simple to produce. He moved to a flat and renovated it to demonstrate his talents. As potential clients walked into his home office, immediately they liked his design and began placing orders. In this way, Jiang started the first private home interior design and decorating company in Shanghai.

Soon many people in the city became interested in redesigning their homes. Jiang expanded his service to include building materials, household fixtures, appliances, and other materials. He opened a large retail store in the central district and contracted suppliers to produce parquet flooring under his company's name (Qianxi). His parquet soon became the most popular choice on the market, and Qianxi became a brand name in its own right. Soon, Qianxi became the No. 1 interior design retailer for homes. Other companies then entered the market trying to capture part of this lucrative business.

The Business Plan

Sensing the growing demand for high quality home improvement in Shanghai, Jiang launched a supermarket to supply everything in home improvement materials—from nails to Finnish saunas. He purchased a shopping mall with

10,000 square meters in the center of town. Customers can get there easily using public transportation. Jiang then invited his five biggest competitors to join him in this supermarket. He theorized that customers would appreciate being able to get everything under one roof. They would have more choices, and the competing companies would be forced to search for goods with better quality and lower prices. They would also have to improve their service. This was a bold approach in China, where the market economy has just begun to take off. Jiang is years ahead of most other Chinese entrepreneurs.

All five of his competitors eagerly agreed to participate, knowing that this supermarket would draw customers. Soon it became known as the place to go for home improvement-related goods. The various merchants also provided services, such as interior design and renovation. The rent they paid to Jiang covered not only the mortgage but also provided a sizable cash flow. Together, these six companies captured most of Shanghai's home interior design market and controlled most of the brand name dealerships. In the year 2000, the sales volume of these six companies was more than RMB 500 million; Qianxi alone had more than RMB 100 million. There are now many booths rented to smaller companies that specialize in certain items such as lighting fixtures or curtains. These smaller stores complement the six main players.

Jiang did not stop there. Looking ahead to the WTO and to Shanghai's rapidly increasing wealth, he established a trade union for interior design and home improvement merchants in Shanghai. This trade union, with Jiang as deputy secretary, established industry standards and a system to protect consumers. He also set up a collective purchasing plan. All six companies can now bargain for better prices from dealers. Jiang invested in a warehouse, teams of logistical staff, and a purchaser to serve this trade union. In fact, he became the main supplier, able to get better prices than would be possible for individual companies. Needless to say,

Jiang has become an interior design tycoon in Shanghai.

Jiang's latest dream is establishing a Web-based interior decorating and home improvement market for the trade union. The Web site—525j.com (525j in Chinese sounds like "I love my home")—connects all the companies in this trade union and lists their latest goods and sales. Further, customers can get exact price quotes on custom-made designs. They no longer need to go to the mall. That is not the end of Jiang's dream. He is now hiring teams of software engineers to do a virtual-reality home design program in three dimensions. Customers can create their own designs on the Web and receive immediate price quotes. Jiang hopes that this approach can increase sales without increasing overhead.

Growth of Business

Jiang started humbly with a 13-square-meter home office. Thirteen years later, he owns a 10,000 square-meter shopping mall and a company of 370 employees with more than RMB 100 million in sales. Clearly, he has established himself as a successful businessman. He has also set the standards in the industry. Each time he has done something new, Jiang has increased his core business yet retained his focus.

Despite all of Jiang's talents, he has never received a visit from the pastoral staff of his church in Shanghai. The churches there seldom tap Christians like Jiang for church ministry. There are only about 40 to 50 full-time pastors for every 100,000 Christians in Shanghai—a 1:2,000 pastor/member ratio. Although Jiang does not have many Christian friends, he is well known as a Christian among his business colleagues, who are almost all non-Christians. Jiang has been looking for Christian teachings on business but has found none.

In business, Jiang bucks common practice and does not give bribes or participate in immoral entertainment. Instead, he focuses on improving his service and coming up with innovative ideas to maintain his advantage. He refuses to take business from the entertainment industry, such as nightclubs, because the Chinese mafia owns much of it. Jiang also eschews the traditional custom of setting up an altar for Chinese folk gods at one of his home interior renovation jobs. Sometimes, however, customers ask that Buddhist monks or Daoist priests conduct ceremonies. Mr. Jiang never sponsors them and makes sure he is elsewhere on such occasions. Because his clients know that Jiang is a Christian, they usually do not mind his absence.

Jiang has been fair to his staff, and the turnover rate is very low. His employees generally believe that the company has a bright future. They take pride in being associated with it. Often, Jiang helps them as personal problems arise. Jiang discovered that one of his branch managers wanted to start his own business. Jiang knew this talented man was being underutilized in his responsibilities with Qianxi. Therefore, Jiang lent him money and gave him enough credit to launch his own company. This new company now complements Jiang's regional branch.

Jiang seeks not to defeat his business competitors but to join them in win-win situations. He looks beyond his own interests and focuses on the whole industry's welfare. His visionary leadership and concern for safe and healthy workplaces in the industry have won him respect from his competitors. Jiang has successfully made alliances with competitors, and together they meet customer needs and enhance the quality of their services—signs of a mature service industry.

Evaluation

Jiang's concern for quality service, combined with his honesty and vision, makes him a successful businessman. He knows how to look beyond his present circumstances and see the wider needs of the industry. He always makes customers his No. 1 priority. He does not feel threatened by competition, nor does he try to fight against it. He sees it as an opportunity to develop a win-win situation for all. His intuitive grasp of trends challenges him to go beyond the present situation even though he is already at the top of his profession.

His business performance is rather impressive, judging from his past 13 years. Jiang does not spread himself too thin by venturing into different fields. Within his area of expertise, he has excelled as the industry leader and the trend setter. Jiang's business has grown continuously, always with new ideas and products to set new industrial standards. With Shanghai continuing to grow rapidly, Jiang will most likely continue contributing innovative ideas. People like Jiang make Shanghai one of the fastest growing industrial cities in the world.

The church in Shanghai is in no position to offer assistance to Jiang or use his gifts for the kingdom. However, Jiang has volunteered and given money for orphanages, homes for the elderly, schools, and scholarships. Jiang does not contribute regularly, but on an ad hoc basis. A taxation officer once asked Jiang why a citizen would give money to charity. The government, the officer said, would take care of everybody's needs. That is why it taxes money donated for private charity work.

Jiang has been looking for a fellowship for Christian business people in Shanghai. The local church, however, is unequipped to provide such teaching or pastoral care. They are lonely sojourners struggling through the complex business world with no spiritual guidance. If Jiang decides to form a Christian business people's network in Shanghai, given his track record, there is little doubt that he will pull it off. Such a fellowship would be the first of its kind in China.

Chapter 6

Business-Turned Mission Model

Some Christians include evangelism in their corporate objectives. They regard themselves as both business people and evangelists. Such a dual identity is evident in the Christians of the Wenzhou areas of Zhejiang Province. Today these Wenzhou Christian merchants have created Christian communities in every province of China. Their presence can also be seen from Prague to Paris, and from New York to Novosibirsk. The following details how Wenzhou Christians proclaim the kingdom through their businesses.

Case Study: The Christian Merchants of Wenzhou

Wenzhou is situated on the southern tip of Zhejiang Province in the southeastern part of China. The local dialect is almost incomprehensible to others. The Wenzhounese are tightly knit, and few outsiders can gain access to the community. It is a hilly place with many people but few farmlands. Because of the lack of farmland, for several hundred years, the Wenzhounese have chosen to make a living as traveling merchants. They usually travel alone, but sometimes in twos or threes, selling household items such as needles, mirrors, and combs from village to village. They may not be home for several months at a stretch. Many of them travel all over the country, even along the Silk Road. They carry not only their goods but also their skills, such as dentistry. For several hundred years, the only dental care that people in Central Asia received was from Wenzhou herbal merchants, who sold analgesic powders and performed tooth extractions in the bazaars. Merchants from Wenzhou had a sizable community in France in the mid-19th century.

Since it instituted the Reform and Open Policy (1980), China has allowed commercial activities after three decades of socialism. The Wenzhounese immediately seized the opportunity and began producing commodities, such as clothing and household appliances. They wanted to meet the demand of peasants who suddenly had more disposable income from the new policy. Carrying their merchandise all over China, they started free markets (as opposed to the state-owned stores), with flexible trading systems such as bargaining and floating prices, depending on supply and demand. Soon Wenzhou became the center of clothing and shoe manufacturing in China, and Wenzhou merchants dominated the free markets in China. Even now, 98 percent of Wenzhou's GDP comes from private enterprises and only 2 percent from SOEs. This is the highest ratio among all Chinese municipalities. As economic conditions have improved, the Wenzhounese manufactured different types of goods to suit the market and established outlets all over China. They, in fact, set consumer trends in China. Since the early 1990s, Wenzhou merchants have extended their reach into Eastern Europe. Now they dominate the two largest commodity markets, in Budapest and Bucharest. Called "the Chinese Jews," they can be found anywhere there is a business opportunity. Overall, the Wenzhounese have perhaps the highest income of any group in China. However, because they try to avoid paying taxes, there are no reliable figures on the extent of their commercial activities.

Wherever they are, the Wenzhounese tend to stick together. They do not mix with other Chinese. This approach to life enables them to preserve their distinct identity. In spite of their widely scattered trading activities, they seldom settle in foreign places, nor do they like to integrate into other local cultures. Wenzhou is their home, a place to return to as often as possible.

Like the itinerant missionary, the traveling merchant has often faced danger, since traveling has been unsafe in many places. Not surprisingly, the Wenzhounese are rather religious in the face of a very uncertain and dangerous way of life. Traditionally, they donate large sums of money to their local temples, or even build new temples, after making it home safely from a long and successful business trip. Wenzhou has one of the highest per-capita concentrations of religious venues in China.

When Christianity arrived in Wenzhou in the mid-19th century, few of the people believed in this new religion. That slowly began to change. After almost a century of intensive efforts by various mission societies, there were perhaps several thousand Christians in Wenzhou in 1950. During the late 1950s and the early 1960s, the government tried to establish Wenzhou as one of the first atheistic zones; it tried to coerce people to recant their faith. Soon religion disappeared from Wenzhou. However, people's Christian faith survived in secret. In the mid-1970s, overseas Christians were able to confirm the presence of a vibrant Christian community there. These Christians had mimeographed copies of the New Testament, and many were sent to labor camps by the authorities. Christianity was once again officially tolerated in 1980, and the Christian community in Wenzhou experienced the fastest growth of all municipalities in China. As of the year 2000, in a population of 7 million, there are about 1 million Christians who belong to the officially recognized church. They have several thousand church buildings and meeting points. There may be perhaps an equal number of Christians in the non-registered churches. Wenzhou boasts the highest concentration of Christians in China, at least in a municipality. The area is called the Jerusalem of China. One can easily spot at least one church in every village or town within Wenzhou.

With such high percentages of both merchants and Christians, one may wonder if there is any relationship. The following case study profiles a group of Wenzhou Christian merchants who did business in Xining, Qinghai Province (a very remote place dominated by Muslims and Tibetan Buddhists in the northwestern part of China). A typical story is told in an interview format.

The Call

Why did you get into business?

Everyone in Wenzhou does business. It is our tradition. We go to school but only until junior high school or senior high school. To become independent, we get out and start our own businesses. This way, we can prove that we are adults. We have limited resources in Wenzhou, so we have to do trading to make a living.

Are you a Christian?

Yes, I am. I have been Christian since I was young. We are baptized in the church. Some of us attend the officially recognized church, and others attend the non-registered church back home.

What does the church teach about evangelism?

We are taught that we have to preach the gospel. It is the duty of all Christians. Our churches back home do much evangelistic work, and they are still growing. No matter where we are, we have to preach the gospel. We also believe that business can help to create more jobs and enhance the livelihoods of many. It is a good thing to do.

The Entrepreneurial Launch

How did you come to Qinghai?

I came here 12 years ago. At that time, there was nothing in this city. So I brought some household lighting fixtures from Wenzhou to sell. I saw a business opportunity and also an opportunity to spread the gospel to others in this remote frontier. I came here alone. The first thing I did was to look for a church.

I then looked at the market here and identified things that I can get from Wenzhou to sell to the locals. Soon I began to expand my range of goods and became the regional retailer for many products. I hired several locals and have a couple of retail shops.

[Other merchants have given similar stories, but they have dealt with different goods such as clothing, building materials, and electric appliances.]

What are the main challenges in your business?

I do not bribe people, because I am a Christian. Therefore, I never get those big government contracts. I deal with smaller business partners. I get business because I give people a good price and good service. It is a very competitive market, so I always have to be on the lookout for opportunities.

What are the difficulties that you have faced?

The major difficulty is lack of capital for large contracts. With more cash flow and capital, I could increase my volume and expand my business much faster. At first, because I do not drink and do not treat my customers to nightclubs, I lost a lot of business. But as time passed, people came to know that I was a Christian. They know now that I am honest and will not cheat them. They like to deal with me rather than with non-Christians. Business is a long-term thing. Honesty and trustworthiness are the keys to business success.

The Business Plan

How did you go about developing your business?

I will usually look at the market and seek some opportunity to introduce goods manufactured in Wenzhou. Since Wenzhou produces many trendy household commodities, I usually have little problem getting them in. However, to continue such trade, I need to constantly monitor the market. I'll also look beyond Xining City [the provincial capital] to the surrounding counties and become the distributor for this region. I am now looking further west to see if there are new markets. Basically, I am market-driven. Wherever the market is, that is where I will go. In fact, this has been the basic business model for Wenzhou merchants.

So far, I am doing rather well here. I am still looking for opportunities to do more business, either with partners or in new markets. Wenzhou merchants like to operate alone, and we have many lone rangers doing different things. At times we cooperate, but only on a project basis. We like to be independent.

Growth of Business

Has your business been growing?

My business so far is profitable. I know of Wenzhou merchants who have lost money in some deals. I have lost money, too. However, in the long run, most of us make money. We don't make a lot of money, but we make enough to live comfortably–both us and those back home. We usually hire locals and train them. In my case, I hired 10 people in my shop.

Wherever we are, we try to hold Christian meetings. We always have worship. When we arrived in Xining, there were only a few people from Wenzhou. None was Christian. That was 12 years ago. Later, a few Wenzhou Christians came. We began to have our own Christian meetings. Now we have two Wenzhou Christian meetings in this city—each attended by 150 every week, more during Christmas. We take turns to preach, and we are all volunteers. Many Wen-zhounese became Christians through us. We also led many of our local workers to Christ. They can't speak our dialects so they go to the local city church for worship. There are many minorities among our staff—Muslims and Tibetans. However, it is difficult to lead them to Christ. So far, all of the new Christians are Han Chinese.

Some of us are now bringing Christ to very remote areas where hitherto no Christian had ever visited. And we also established Christian meetings in our homes and shops in those places. Very often, we are the only Christians gathering in those towns. For example, the only Christian worship place in Lhasa, Tibet, is in the home of a Wenzhou merchant. The local government usually tolerates us, because we bring economic prosperity. There is one important point that differs from our meetings back home. At home, we make a point of separating those who meet at the officially recognized churches and those who meet at the non-registered churches. Out in this place, we do not make any distinctions among ourselves. We are just Christians who long for fellowship.

We are well known in the business community for our faith. Our business practices are clean—no bribes, no kickbacks, and no expensive entertainment. We do give gifts, but only in festival seasons to maintain good relationships. We do not associate such gifts with particular business deals. We uphold the biblical principle of fairness. Our workers seem to respect us, as do our business partners. We teach our staff and we have standards for them to follow. We treat them in a fair and respectful way. The turnover among our staff is very low, and they treasure the jobs we offer them.

Evaluation

From a business perspective, the Christian merchants from Wenzhou are individual entrepreneurs. They penetrate the most hard-to-reach frontiers, bringing not only goods but economic prosperity. They like to be pioneers and to explore untapped markets. They emphasize fairness, which enables them to build their business networks. They operate small businesses with simple structures and high degrees of flexibility to suit the dynamics of the market.

Most of their businesses succeed. Wenzhou merchants are the best small-business people in China. They fit right into the current economic trend—the gradual opening of the country to a market economy, and the unleashing of the economic potential of untapped markets.

Wherever these Wenzhou Christian merchants go, they

establish their Christian witness through zealous evangelism. In their vocations, they manifest honesty and hard work. These values are clearly a reflection of their Christian faith. This combination of faith and business makes them perhaps the best missionaries to the unreached in China. However, their strong provincial identity—Wenzhounese—prohibits them from interacting with local Christians, beyond their generous financial support.

As China opens up its western frontier for economic development, there are huge business opportunities for these merchants. They are used to entering challenging areas. They specialize in household commodities in Eastern Europe. Many of them go to Europe illegally. In fact, the largest group of illegal Chinese immigrants to Europe is the Wenzhounese, and the number is growing. Their penetrative power, flexibility, and resilient spirit enable them to crack virtually any country that denies entry to Western merchants.

Chapter 7

Bridgehead Model

There are Christians from outside China who feel called to share the gospel in China, despite the fact that China denies missionary entry. In response, many take on different kinds of roles. One of the common roles is that of a business person, because entrepreneurs are most welcome by the Chinese government. The following case describes a Christian who is faithfully following the call of God to become a businessman in China for the sake of the gospel.

Case Study: Mr. Ming-to Shing and the Hong Kong Channel

Mr. Ming-to Shing (hereafter referred to as MT) comes from a long line of Christians. His grandmother's foster mother was an American missionary who studied at Moody Bible Institute. This American missionary worked among the fishermen and the poor living in river junks in northern Guangdong Province during the 1930s and 1940s. His mother had been a Bible woman (pastor) who later came to Hong Kong. Although his grandfather was a scholar, because of poverty and social turbulence, MT's father had no opportunity to get an education. His father nevertheless was a devoted Christian. Once he set a goal, he pursued it at all costs. This character trait influenced MT as he grew up.

During the 1960s, many people in Hong Kong lived in extreme poverty. MT's family, with seven children, was impoverished. Mrs. Shing had a meager income as a Bible woman. Mr. Shing had no professional skills, so he worked as a hawker on the street. Street peddling in Hong Kong was illegal under British colonial law, and hawkers had to pay bribes to both the police and gangsters. A hawker had to be a good runner, because the police constantly chased him. There was no steady income, and the authorities could confiscate hawkers' goods whenever they wanted. Their profession had zero social respectability and was reserved for those who had no other options. Therefore, Mr. and Mrs. Shing prayed that their children would get respectable professions with steady incomes, as doctors or teachers. Eventually, three of them became teachers, and three others entered medicine. In fact, they all fulfilled the prayerful wishes of the Shings—all except for MT.

The Call

In the summer of 1969, 14-year-old MT went to a Christian camp. At the time, he attended a church that belonged to the Oriental Mission to the Boat People, which had a fundamentalist doctrine. It did not believe in signs and wonders or any charismatic manifestations, although it did believe in exorcisms. (MT had witnessed several of them.) One clear day, MT heard what he felt was a voice from God telling him, "Your mission field is China; your profession is a businessman; and you will become a movie director."

This calling presented some huge problems for MT. His mother was a pastor in the same non-charismatic mission. MT had never even been in a theater. The family wanted MT to take up a "respectable profession." They saw business as a sign of worldliness and greed.

To prepare himself for what he firmly believed was God's calling, MT began to learn Mandarin. This is the predominant dialect in China, but it was completely unpopular in Hong Kong. MT became a laughing stock at school for learning Mandarin from a mathematics teacher. His family completely rejected his calling as an entrepreneur and movie director. Nevertheless, he pressed on. After earning a degree in sociology, MT entered the first movie director training program offered by TVB, Hong Kong's largest television station.

MT knew that he had to save money before he could begin his business. He also knew that the only way to get into China for evangelistic work was as a businessman. After working for a couple of years, he started a small video production studio. After 10 years of work in Hong Kong, he had enough money to start a VHS videotape duplication business in China.

The Entrepreneurial Launch

MT developed a joint-venture partnership with a small VHS duplication facility in China. The Chinese partner, with 40 employees, manufactures video copies of masters produced in MT's Hong Kong studio. This factory enables MT to establish media contacts and win video production contracts. MT saw that there were growing numbers of Chinese businessmen who spent half of their time on the road, and he thought he could reach them with the gospel. To do so, he bought a channel that was reaching 20,000 hotel rooms. MT's hotel channel may soon be the first medium to bring the gospel to these itinerant business people.

In fact, MT's most difficult trials have come from his family and church. They still have a hard time accepting his calling as a businessman-missionary. Nonetheless, he presses on. MT makes a point of telling his Chinese counterparts that he is a Christian. Therefore, they do not expect him to give bribes or gifts. He avoids all nightclubs and karaoke bars. Although his scruples have cost him a lot of business, MT remains positive. He believes that if God does not want him to make certain deals, it will be all right. MT has turned down lucrative opportunities proffered by Marlboro and by a nightclub in Macao where gambling and prostitution are rife. When business colleagues express their surprise at these countercultural decisions, MT takes the opportunity to share his faith.

The Business Plan

MT's plan is simple. One, he conducts business with one purpose in mind—to contact Chinese business people and officials in order to share the gospel with them. Two, the business has to be economically viable. Three, his business must not dishonor God. Four, he does not worry about the business too much, because God owns it. So far, MT has been following these principles with remarkable success. His business is growing, and he will soon launch a hotel channel with programs that will feed into thousands of hotel rooms in China. He has been able to reject business proposals that contradict his beliefs. Above all, he has led many to Christ.

MT has developed a method he calls "Grace Evangelism." Whenever he meets with business associates and government officials in China for lunch or dinner, he tells them that as a Christian, he says grace before meals. Usually his companions, out of courtesy or curiosity, ask him to go ahead. MT then produces a lengthy prayer that includes the basics of the gospel. After this, not surprisingly, the conversation at the table centers on religion and faith. MT elaborates more on the gospel as necessary, and responses are generally positive. Many of the officials admit that they have nothing to believe in, but they say Christianity conflicts with their positions in the Communist Party. However, many say they hope their children will embrace Christianity. Some do become Christians, however, and MT takes them to the local church for further instruction and, eventually, baptism.

Growth of Business

MT employs a production crew in Hong Kong and works in a joint venture with a Chinese factory in VHS duplication. With strong demand for such services, MT has expanded his business into other media platform such as the Internet and private TV channels. He has been running these businesses in Hong Kong and is looking for the right opportunity to start them in China.

MT has been a successful evangelist among Chinese business colleagues. Many have turned to Christ through his witness. He also has shared the gospel with factory workers. Because these workers are mostly on short-term contracts, there are always new ones being exposed to the gospel. Some management team members are Christians as well. Whenever he visits the factory, he organizes Bible studies for the Christians. The Christian staff members of this factory attend the local government-recognized church, which MT supports generously.

MT also supports some charities, such as a Christian-operated orphanage in Guangxi Province. He organizes the Full Gospel Business People Shenzhen (China) chapter for both expatriate and local Christian business people. He is now developing a former leprosy asylum camp to train peasants both in agricultural techniques and in Christian formation. So far, however, MT has not found any suitable partners among the local Christian communities. This project will take a holistic approach to development, combining small business and Christian discipleship.

When MT started his business, his employees took advantage of him because he was a Christian. For example, many demanded that MT be "compassionate" and tolerate even their wrongdoings. Some abused MT's good will and cheated him. As he became wiser, MT toughened his personnel management style. He now safeguards his company's interests and refuses extra demands from the employees. He admits that he is still learning in this area.

Evaluation

MT's business in China is still a small operation, with a few dozen staff members. However, as he enters the hotel channel business, there is much potential for growth. He will have access to many thousands of Chinese business people who travel extensively in the country. He will be able to sell advertisements, promote particular products, and receive sponsorships. He already has a good logistical support team in Hong Kong. It is a low overhead, low risk, high yield business.

Until now, MT's ministry has been quite effective through his personal witnessing. As he begins the hotel channel, he has to look for appropriate programs that can, on the one hand, promote Christian values, and, on the other hand, stay within Chinese law, which prohibits the propagation of religion in public, including hotels. A trained film director, he wants to produce tailor-made programs for his target group. Further, MT believes this channel can be a platform to gather Chinese Christian business people, scattered throughout the country, into an informal network.

MT also believes that Chinese businessmen can bring the gospel to areas inaccessible to others, such as the Muslim areas in the northwest. He believes that merchants can most effectively go to those places. Generally, local governments welcome such people but are skeptical of others. Given the right opportunity, he wants to organize Christian business people to expand the kingdom of God. So far, MT has followed his calling for 32 years. He is poised to reach a new level of business and ministry in China.

Chapter 8

Communal Living Model

Most Chinese Christian entrepreneurs employ non-Christians in their businesses, since Christians are a minority in China. The only visible community of Christians in China is the church. However, a few enterprises have mostly Christians working in them. These Christian communities are alternative forms of Christian corporate witness that interface intimately with all areas of life. Below is the story of a group of Christians who are running a successful business and glorifying the name of God in a place where Christianity is virtually unknown.

Case Study: The Hua Xia Group

In the 1920s, a group of Chinese Christians formed a farming community called the "Jesus Family" in northern China. Similar to the Amish in the United States, it was an indigenous, socially self-contained, self-sustaining community with a strong sense of ideal Christianity. The government, however, disbanded this Jesus Family movement in the 1950s. Yet the ideal was not extinguished. In the mid-1990s, a Christian couple started a restaurant and hotel business in northern China that has grown to include 400 Christian employees living together as a family. This business community, called the Hua Xia Group, has a corporate objective: "Whenever we start a new enterprise (business), we bless that particular place." The mission statement is: "To provide high quality food and service, to respect customers and staff, and to help resolve various social problems, including environmental issues."

The Hua Xia Group is one of the most successful private enterprises in northern China, and its founder is no stranger to talk shows and magazines. When people ask why his business is so successful, he simply says that the group follows Christian principles and that its success is nothing but the grace of God. Indeed, Hua Xia's prosperity has attracted many entrepreneurs trying to learn its secret. As they observe Hua Xia's daily operation, they find out that there is really no trade secret except that the employees are either sincere Christians, or at least committed to following the teachings of the Bible in their daily lives.

The Beginning

Mr. Fung Hai's mother was a Buddhist. His father was a Communist Party member serving in the army. After high school, Fung joined an army-operated lumber company in a small city about 36 miles from Shangyang, the capital of Liaoning Province. Finding no challenges and seeing no future in this state-owned company, Fung went to Shangyang in 1991 and got a position as a purchaser for a small restaurant. A local businessman who was partnering with a Hong Kong merchant ran it. Fung immediately sensed the management difference between China's state-owned enterprise and the foreign company, and he tried to learn as much as he could.

After a year, the owner offered Fung and the manager, a certain Miss Han Miling, the opportunity to run the whole restaurant on a contract basis. They would receive a bonus if the restaurant exceeded a certain sales volume. The owner felt comfortable letting these two run his business. He knew they did not get along well and would be sure to check on each other.

Han came from neighboring Jilin Province, where her parents had suffered greatly during the Cultural Revolution.

One day in the early 1980s, desperate and hopeless, they walked by a church and were attracted by hymn singing. As the couple sat down, they were deeply touched by the hymn "What a Friend We Have in Jesus." They immediately knew that this was what they needed. Government employees, they secretly accepted the Christian faith. They began to tell their daughter about their new beliefs but did not take her to church. Later, Han went to Shangyang to study orthopedics. Han's mother began praying for her daughter to find a husband. During Han's final year, she took a part-time job at the restaurant to earn some extra income. Later, she worked as the full-time floor manager.

While Han and Fung worked together as uneasy business partners, Han's mother came and visited her daughter. Immediately she felt that Fung was the answer to her prayer, and she gave him a Bible. Proverbs quickly caught his attention, and he read it all night, believing that this was the path he should follow. To this point he had never even heard of Christianity, and he did not know if there was a church in town. Fung used all his spare time to study the Bible. He felt that the Word cleansed his heart and mind, and he experienced an uplifting of his soul. Meanwhile, Han also had become interested in the Christian faith as well. Soon both became Christians and found a local church with help from Han's mother. Because they were the only young people in the church, the pastor gave them much personal guidance. Their interpersonal conflicts became a thing of the past, and every morning they prayed for the day's work. Suddenly, the restaurant's sales volume jumped from RMB10,000 a day to RMB16,000-18,000 a day. At the same time, the neighboring restaurants were struggling. Han and Fung knew this was God's blessing, not the result of their efforts. After a period of courtship, they married. Even though they had no starting capital, they decided to launch their own business. Both felt God's call to be witnesses in business. Fung had even had a dream in which he invited Jesus to dine at his restaurant. He took it as a sign that he should be in the restaurant business.

The Entrepreneurial Launch

One day a customer who was impressed with them said he had a newly renovated restaurant (worth RMB 2 million) they could run if they would pay RMB 270,000 in rent for the first two years. It was a very good deal, but they simply did not have the money. Later, this customer returned and said: "I do not know why I made this decision. I do not know you, but I am willing to trust you. You can have my restaurant to run for two years, and you do not have to pay me the two years' rent now. Just pay me at the end of two years." They could not refuse such a God-given opportunity. Both had prayed for this so that they could share Christ with customers—people who would not normally come to church to hear the gospel.

As they began, business was poor, and they had many debts to suppliers. At one point, they had saved RMB 30,000 but had to pay RMB 30,000 within a week to creditors. Then three Christians from a local church asked them to contribute that amount to the building fund. This young couple struggled. Should they pay the business debt or donate the money to the church? Both felt that their business belonged to God, not to them. With a certain degree of both reluctance and joyfulness, they handed the money to the Christians. The next day, they earnestly prayed for the business.

On an average day, they would net about RMB 3,000. They asked for RMB 5,000. To their surprise, the restaurant was flooded with people, and it took in RMB 7,800. That evening, the employees gathered to give thanks. Brisk business days continued. The restaurant began holding morning devotionals and evening Bible studies, which became the hallmark of the Hua Xia Group. The Fungs learned their first important lesson in Christian business—everything they have belongs to God, not to them. They are merely stewards of God's wealth. Therefore, they see the business as an extension of the kingdom of God.

In 1995, a larger restaurant needing renovation went out of business. The Fungs were able to buy it, and they recruited young people from the church to run it. Many people in the town laughed at them because this restaurant had been a perennial money-loser for a number of owners. Because it was situated in a small alley with no parking space, it could not attract wealthy customers. The city's economic climate was worsening, as many state owned enterprises had collapsed. When the Fungs took over, it was late fall and impossible to finish the renovation before winter. The interior would be ruined by cold weather and snow. The Fungs and all the employees prayed every day as they started the renovation work. That winter, Shangyang City had the warmest fall on record. Usually the snow would come in mid-October, but that year the snow came a few days before Christmas Eve. The first flakes fell just one minute after the last piece of renovation work was completed on the front door. The restaurant opened on Christmas Day, a tradition that they managed to follow at the openings of their subsequent businesses.

This restaurant, the flagship of the Hua Xia Group, has become a legend in the city. Although it is in a back alley, many people come. In just six months, the restaurant was packed every night. Many restaurants use many sales gimmicks such as discounts, free drinks, beautiful and flirty waitresses, kickbacks for corporate accounts, and gifts to boost business. The Hua Xia restaurant uses none of them. It simply maintains its image of honesty and fairness. Every customer receives respectful and polite service. The waiters and waitresses never push expensive dishes or favor one brand of drink over another. Customers are encouraged to make their own choices. People have to wait one to two hours for a seat if they do not call ahead for reservations. Meanwhile, dozens of nearby restaurants with better ambience and discount deals are half empty.

Two years later, the Fungs opened a food court in the city center and a resort hotel and restaurant 18 miles from the city. The hotel restaurant is so popular, many customers drive for an hour through heavy snowstorms just for dinner.

They often have to call for help to tow their cars out of highway ditches.

A year ago, the couple invested RMB 500,000 to start two Christian Web sites, but the government closed them down. Today, they have more than 480 employees, two restaurants, a resort hotel, a school, a fish farm, a horse ranch, a training school for new employees, and a publishing house.

The Business Plan

The corporate mission objective of the Hua Xia Group states: "Whenever we start a new enterprise, we bless that particular place." It carries out its mission by consciously living by Christian values and employing young Christians or young people from Christian families. The company trains them in biblical studies and professional skills. The emphasis is on Christian character formation—honesty, charity, and cleanliness. With a batch of newly trained staff, the company opens new businesses with veteran managers from Hua Xia. Quality service and good customer relations are considered the keys to their business success.

The employees live at a company dormitory, complete with recreation amenities. Those who get married (and most who do choose spouses in the community) have their weddings organized and paid for by Hua Xia. Married couples receive well-furnished apartments provided by the company. Hua Xia also runs a free kindergarten as well as recreation programs for employees' children. Hua Xia also holds anti-smoking campaigns among the staff. Hua Xia employees experience life almost as a religious community, with daily morning devotions and evening worship. They are divided into teams led by managers, who are also spiritual mentors.

Hua Xia's restaurants provide a peaceful setting with quality food and service. Further, they try hard to bless their neighbors through assistance for flood victims, visits to nursing homes, sports activities for local youths, and an emphasis on healthy environments. When the North Atlantic Treaty Organization bombed Belgrade, including the Chinese

Embassy, several years ago, many civilians were injured or killed. Hua Xia donated money for relief work. The company also gives Bibles and gospel tracts to customers, organizes Christmas caroling, and takes prayer requests from customers. Hua Xia has funded many church buildings and pastoral training projects. In short, Hua Xia wants to develop a business group that becomes a blessing to the employees, neighbors, and customers.

Making money and satisfying the needs of the employees, customers, and neighbors seem impossible. Yet the result so far is encouraging. Hua Xia is still expanding and all of its businesses are prospering. Few employees feel any pressure to participate in so many religious activities. Instead, they are proud to be Hua Xia employees and proud of the company's Christian culture. They make no attempt to hide their faith. On the contrary, they try to express it as much as possible. Their resort hotel may be the only hotel in China that places free copies of the Bible in each room. It also places Chinese couplets with Christian messages on the guest room doors. Not surprisingly, this evangelistic boldness has gotten the company into trouble with authorities. For example, restaurant employees used to distribute Bibles to guests before the police banned this practice. So now they just leave a few copies on the counter for customers to "steal."

Many customers return to the restaurants over and over, saying there is a special atmosphere of peace. Quarreling families usually make peace among themselves at the table. Most Chinese business deals get closed not in company boardrooms but in restaurants. Employees pray that all customers will be blessed as they enter the restaurants, and it seems that God honors their prayers. Many business people say they cannot close deals at other places as they can at Hua Xia. Staff members remember specific customer requests and will even follow up. Several customers experienced miraculous healing through these prayers and became Christians.

However, some customers take advantage of restaurant employees and make unreasonable demands, especially after getting drunk. While employees will not quarrel with them, other customers sometimes will rebuke the troublemakers. In almost every single case, the troublemakers come back and apologize. However, dealing with opportunistic staff members is more difficult. Some lie to the company (for example, claiming a sick parent) to get an advance paycheck. Others take extra food or supplies for personal use. Many times Hua Xia will tolerate these people and look for signs of repentance. For repeated offenders, however, Hua Xia will fire them and openly announce their wrongdoings. Some are fired for violating the company's community moral code—e.g., cohabitation without formal marriage. So far, the disciplinary cases have been few and far between.

Hua Xia's community outreach projects are well received by the neighbors. Hua Xia has been in the public media often as one of the few private enterprises able to make a profit and help the needy. Almost all members of the state-controlled media have deliberately downplayed Hua Xia's Christian character, but it is impossible to hide its clear Christian beacon shining forth.

Growth of Business

The Hua Xia enterprise employs more than 480 staff members, and the number is growing. Most of them hail from rural areas and came without employment skills. They must go through several months of catering training at Hua Xia's own training institute to become skilled workers. Although they receive relatively low salaries, good employee benefits encourage them to stay.

Hua Xia is making a visible progress in expanding the kingdom of God. Many new staff members who are sent by Christian parents make commitments to Christ during their training periods. Many customers are attracted to Christianity as they interact with employees. Local churches usually get newcomers introduced by Hua Xia. Meanwhile, Fung has been newly ordained as an elder in his church. Since September 2001, he has been attending the graduate division of the Jining Theological Seminary in Nanjing. The Hua Xia Group has been praying that some of its staff members enter pastoral ministry. Currently the company does not have a comprehensive staff development program, but has relied on piecemeal short-term Christian character-building Bible studies. It has just hired a staff development manager from the United States (a minister of the Mennonite Church) as its de facto chaplain.

In its business conduct, the Hua Xia Group makes it clear that it upholds Christian values. Restaurants in China generally hire beautiful young ladies, dressed seductively, to flirt with customers. Many of these restaurants even operate "karaoke rooms," which, in fact, are brothels. Hua Xia shuns this approach. Its waitresses look wholesome and wear almost no makeup. They treat guests with heart-felt warmth. Customers comment that these waitresses are like their sisters. Their presence arouses not sexual desire but a family-like atmosphere. Therefore, customers naturally respond respectfully. In fact, if a businessman tells his wife that he is entertaining clients at Hua Xia, she usually feels confident that her husband is not fooling around behind her back. A morally clean restaurant is a rarity in China. Yet this is the public impression of Hua Xia.

Hua Xia is trying to set industrial standards in other areas as well. There are many counterfeit goods in China, especially wine and liquors. Garbage collectors will pay restaurants a premium for empty wine and liquor bottles. A cognac bottle will fetch $3, for example. Often these collectors sell the bottles to counterfeit winemakers who refill them with cheap substitutes. Virtually every restaurant in a city participates in the illicit trade. Hua Xia, however, has given explicit orders to staffers to break every empty wine and liquor bottle. There are three reasons: (1) The bottle will not be used for counterfeit wine, which may harm the consumer; (2) the restaurant will not encourage the counterfeit industry; and (3) people will have faith in the restaurant industry.

Not every moral decision is so clear, however. China's business environment has many gray areas, because it is a system of rule by law rather than a rule of law. Nearly every business evades some taxes and fees. One has to keep in mind that thousands of laws and regulations are in conflict with each other. They are often introduced by self-serving government bureaucrats. Often a law is a tool not to protect individual rights but to advance an official's interest. It is impossible or impractical to keep them all. Facing this conundrum, Hua Xia follows social norms rather than the letter of the law. That is, if everybody else pays a certain fee or tax, then Hua Xia will pay. If nobody pays, it will not.

Many investors and venture capitalists have asked Hua Xia to enter joint ventures or develop branches in different cities. Fung tells them all that he does not want partners or capital investment. His only partner is God. He has no need for more capital, because if God wants Hua Xia to grow, he will do so. Fung says that he already has a good partner, and that he is just a manager for this silent partner from heaven.

Some are willing to pay Fung handsomely to share his secret or teach the Hua Xia spirit. Many even send in teams of managers to observe Hua Xia's operation to learn its trade secret. Fung's answer is simple. He welcomes all to inspect his enterprise but says that the only recipe is total commitment to God. Prayer is his only secret weapon. Fung says the business—whether it succeeds or fails—belongs to God, not to him. Many think that Fung is hiding something. Others think he is crazy. Yet they cannot dismiss the reality that Hua Xia is a successful and growing enterprise.

Evaluation

Hua Xia runs an ethical business. Its ethical stance actually draws customers. The company seems to have found a market niche. Its phenomenal business performance can be explained in part by the youthfulness of both the market and the enterprise itself. Hua Xia has not yet made a clear distinction between business and ministry; there is every attempt to merge them. So far they have not conflicted. We do not have sufficient data or experience to challenge such a model. We need to observe Hua Xia longer before making an evaluation. For example, what happens when the staff grows older and family interests start to conflict with business interests? What happens if there are scandals among the top leaders? What if a senior leader lapses in his or her faith? So far, staff members are young and enthusiastic, motivated by their idealism and fueled by their success.

Hua Xia, still in its infancy stage, is making good progress, but it has yet to firm up its corporate culture or to formulate a long-term objective. Its ideals for ministry and business are riding on the vision of the founders. This is both a strength and a weakness. Fung and Han still make all the major decisions and can, if they wish, exercise absolute control. They behave like the patriarch and matriarch of a big tribe or a clan populated almost exclusively by young children.

Hua Xia is a promising enterprise that seems to mirror the successful Jesus Family rural community model (1930– 1950), but in a modern, urban context. However, until Hua Xia moves from the autocratic leadership of its founders to a more democratic style of corporate management, it cannot claim to be a holistic model for others to emulate.

Chapter 9

Ecclesiastical Self-Supporting Model

The church in China in general is impoverished. The government prohibits it from collecting offerings during services. Meager donations from believers are often not sufficient to sustain church operations. Intensifying the problem, government regulations restrict the church from receiving donations from overseas. Therefore, many churches try to run businesses to sustain themselves financially. While some businesses have succeeded, many more have been failures through mismanagement. For churches that actually make money, wealth can become a corrosive agent that destroys the spiritual integrity of the pastoral staff. The following case, however, is noteworthy. This church-based enterprise has brought financial resources to the church and the gospel to the people.

Case Study: The Love of Jesus through Social Service

The Protestant church ins China follows a "Three-Self" ecclesiastical principle. It must be self-administering, self-supporting, and self-propagating. With China's resurgence of nationalism beginning in the early 1920s, the church has also been caught up in this sociopolitical trend. Church leaders first advocated the "Three-Self" principle during the 1930s, when most were under the control of foreign mission boards. They tried to decrease their financial reliance on foreign mission agencies and place their own people in leadership positions. However, this experiment floundered, as China was caught in various wars until 1949, when the communists consolidated their power.

The government of the People's Republic of China endorsed the Three-Self principle in the hope that it would help the church to be more nationalistic. Soon, many church-operated institutions such as schools and hospitals were nationalized and foreign support was cut off. These institutions, however, could not financially support themselves. Quite a number of clergymen lost their jobs, and many churches closed. Only those that could support themselves survived.

When churches reopened in the 1980s, they still had to follow the Three-Self principle. For many churches, self-support is as challenging as ever. The only income they get is from the rental of their properties, supplemented by donations from believers. However, rural Christians, who comprise a large percentage of the church, are usually poor. Not only do they have little to give, they often need church charity themselves.

During the late 1980s, churches began advocating business involvement to pay the bills. Some congregations ran cake shops. Others operated clothing stores. A few went into commodity trading, the restaurant business, and farming. Most lost money due to mismanagement or inexperience. Many pastoral resources got sucked into business while believers suffered from lack of pastoral care. People began to question whether the church should be running businesses. If not, the question remained: How can the church survive financially with so many poor Christians under its care?

The following two enterprises were run both as for-profit businesses and as outreach programs. The church in Qingyuan Prefecture—the poorest region in Guangdong Province—has about 6,000 Christians scattered in seven northern counties. Before 1949, Baptists, the Assemblies of God, Lutherans, and Methodists operated churches, schools, and hospitals or clinics in the region. All the churches were merged into one during the late 1950s, and the smaller chapels or preaching points in remote places were closed due to the lack of pastors and support. Soon, all church activity was banned during the Cultural Revolution.

In the early 1980s, the provincial church reopened in a newly built five-story building. It was funded both from government compensation for confiscated church properties and through donations from Hong Kong. Looking for a way to serve the community, church leaders began to realize that not many day-care or kindergarten services were available. Traditionally individual working units operated these facilities. However, an increasing influx of rural workers and self-employed proprietors made that approach insufficient. The church saw this need as an opportunity to extend its influence into the community. No more would its activity be confined strictly within its four walls, as government policy had decreed. In 1989, the church opened a kindergarten on its second and third floors.

Ji Ai Kindergarten

During its first two years, the Ji Ai (Love of Jesus) Kindergarten had a headmaster who did not do the job properly. In 1991, the church appointed Ms. Yan, a Christian who had worked with kindergartens for more than two decades, to take over. Within two years, this school became one of the best kindergartens in the community. The school does not charge high fees, and yet staff members are very caring toward the children. The monthly rent the school pays the church became its major revenue source.

Under the leadership of Ms. Yan, all teachers must take introductory lessons in Christianity. The curriculum is government-provided, but the school has some discretion in teaching Christian songs. Children are also allowed to perform special programs at the church during Christmas and Easter. However , several teachers who belonged to the Communist Youth League opposed the church's religious influence over the school. They wanted to organize a branch at the school. The school simply fired them. Now several teachers have accepted the Christian faith, and teachers have organized a special choir to sing hymns.

Parents like to send their children to this school because they trust the church. Some had never entered a church until they started taking their children to this school. Several parents now attend Sunday services, and some have joined the church. Church groups from Hong Kong provide special seminars to parents—such as a pediatric care workshop—as part of the church's outreach program. The Ji Ai Kindergarten became a well-known city institution.

However, the government decided to develop a suburban area from a patch of farmland as the new town center. In one year, the school's student population dropped from 100-plus to less than a few dozen. The church then launched an ambitious plan—to build a kindergarten in the heart of the new town center. Since the area is a new municipality, it had no Religious Affairs Bureau or church. Church leaders saw an opportunity to establish a kindergarten with a large school hall that could also be used as a church building. Using their own money, the Christians dedicated a new kindergarten complex in March 2001. The new Ji Ai Kindergarten again has more than 100 students, but leaders expect that enrollment will increase as more people move into the township. The facility has capacity for 300 children.

The kindergarten is completely church-owned. It is both a social service and a commercial enterprise. The church laid out quite a sum for the school complex, but it will receive steady monthly rental income from the school. The school hall can be used as a church once the government approves it. School rental payments are expected to increase as the school grows.

Ji Ai Medical Clinic

Since the early 1990s, the Chinese government has gradually privatized medical service and allowed private medical clinics to compete with generally inefficient government clinics. This does not mean that patient costs always go down, however. Stripped of government subsidies, government clinics may charge patients extra fees to increase their incomes. In this kind of situation, people opt for affordable and reliable medical service. The church in Qingyuan saw this as an opportunity to share the love of God holistically with the community.

One church member is a retired pediatrician who enjoys a high reputation in the city. The church purchased a store, converted it into a clinic, and invited this pediatrician, Dr. Yan, to head the clinic. Dr. Yan is the father of Ms. Yan, the headmistress of the kindergarten. Dr. Yan's father, Rev. Yan, was a famous pastor in the Guangdong area and used to be the minister at the Qingyuan Assembly of God church before 1949. Dr. Yan felt that it was his spiritual obligation to serve the church through his profession. Dr. Yan's youngest daughter, also a physician, later joined her father at the clinic. The clinic then hired a nurse, a pharmacist, and a clerk. All three of these staff members were not Christians at the time, but eventually they all accepted the gospel. Currently the clinic has six staff members. Five of them are Christians, and the sixth is a spiritual seeker.

Soon the clinic became well known for its service. Area people willingly line up for a couple of hours to see a doctor. Unlike other operations in China, the clinic does not prescribe unnecessary medication and charges the patient only the government-established minimum consultation fee. Because of its popularity, this clinic generates a modest profit. Each month it pays the church a set rental fee. At the end of each year, it divides its annual profit into three portions: 60 percent to the church, 20 percent as a bonus to the staff, and 20 percent to reinvest in medical equipment. Some Christian medical groups in Hong Kong also contribute medicine, equipment, and staff resources.

Both the kindergarten and the clinic generate much-needed income for the Qingyuan church, because donations from local Christians, mostly peasants, are minimal. Without the steady income, it would be extremely difficult for the church to care for more than a dozen rural Christian communities within this prefecture. Not only have these two enterprises generated financial resources for the church, but they also bring the gospel out of the church compound and into the community. For many people, the first or the only contact they will have with the church is through the clinic or the kindergarten. The Qingyuan church operates these two businesses both to make money and to witness to the gospel. It utilizes its own resources to meet the needs of the community. In a restricted-access country such as China, self-sustaining, holistic ministries such as kindergartens and clinics are powerful agents for showing God's love.

Conclusion

China formally entered the World Trade Organization on December 10, 2001. This date marks the beginning of revolutionary sociopolitical changes that promise to be no less dramatic than when China adopted socialism in 1949. China's WTO entry will not only transform China from a socialist to a market-oriented economy, it will also change it from an authoritarian communist state to a pragmatic autocracy. China will gradually open almost all of its domestic market to foreign investors while entering the global economic arena on equal footing with other WTO nations. China is emerging from behind the bamboo curtain and coming into the spotlight of the international community. China is regaining its international prominence.

On the domestic side, the Chinese citizens can have their own passports. Amazingly, they can leave the country whenever they wish as long as they can obtain entrance visas to other nations. Similarly, increasing numbers of foreigners will be able to visit China. They will enjoy simpler application procedures. Chinese authorities will gradually ease the residential registration systems to accommodate the movement of skilled laborers within the country. Chinese citizens will be better able to choose where they live. They will be able to start their own businesses or seek employment with companies of their choice, exercising their competitive skills. They will have more freedom and opportunities than ever before. They, rather than government bureaucrats, will be able decide their career destinies. In short, China will never be the same.

Such inevitable social and economic changes will pose challenges for the Chinese government in three critical areas: economic polarization, national stability, and social morality.

First, on the economic front, the WTO entry will present advantages in certain sectors such as finance, service, light industry, and high tech. More direct foreign investment will pour into these areas and will increase exports from these sectors. Private enterprises—domestic or foreign—will come out with highly competitive goods in an open market.

However, the WTO will lead to cheaper imports of agricultural goods and heavy industry products that will probably hurt the livelihoods of millions of Chinese workers. China has about five years to lift the trade barriers that have protected these sectors. Since many small farms will not be competitive, China needs to find jobs for up to 200 million agricultural workers. Further, about 50 million employees of obsolete SOEs will lose their jobs. Although there will be new jobs created with China's huge commercial potential, it is highly questionable that these surplus laborers will be able to fill the new jobs, which will demand a high level of specific skills and knowledge. Some sectors will likely grow richer and others poorer, leading to undesirable social tensions that may discredit the ostensibly socialist government.

In compliance with the WTO's principle of fair competition, China's accession presumes a relatively reliable legal system. Yet one of the foremost sociopolitical issues in China is corruption. The vast numbers of bureaucrats, a legacy from the planned economic system, may not quickly relinquish their power. Many *apparatchiks* in several states of the former Soviet Union and Eastern Europe enriched themselves and brought discredit to the free market in the chaotic transition from communism. Can China's administrative and legal reforms keep up? If not, will China lapse into a traditional Third World dictatorship, where corruption is the norm and wealth is concentrated in the hands of the elite, resulting in the further widening of economic gaps between the rich and the poor? The central government faces a dilemma. It needs to slash powers from many officials and ministries, yet it requires the support of these same officials to keep the Party in power.

Second, the WTO accession will cause social and structural changes. Population migration, from poor to rich and from rural to urban areas, will lead to a highly dynamic society. The social security system, previously provided by the SOEs or other government units, presumes a static social environment. However, China is heading toward a personalized social security system. Private medical and pension plans will probably become the norm. Each local government will have to find its own resources to meet local social security needs. High-income professionals and well-off regions may well welcome such a change. However, the government will need to expend massive resources in a whole new social welfare system for the poorer regions and the low-income classes. Otherwise, it can expect destabilizing social unrest.

Regional differences will compound the resource discrepancy. The government's ambitious project to develop the west requires not only massive government spending on infrastructure, but also investment from the business sector. The thinking is that this infrastructure is just a means to attract investment from the private sector. Will there be enough commercial investment in the west to close the economic gap between west and east? Can the government muster incentives for business investments in the west without distorting the emerging market? How can the government maintain the stability and unity of the regions without gumming up the economy?

Third, there is an appalling lack of business ethics in China. The most senior government trade official has raised the alarm on this issue. This is far from surprising, of course, given that China has been moving toward capitalism from an aggressive anti-capitalist stance for only about 20 years.

China's private sector has yet to find a viable model for business practices. One of the major obstacles foreign investors grapple with is a lack of credibility among Chinese enterprises. Many are basically after quick profits and do not have a long-term business vision. This is largely due to the unstable business environment over the past two decades. However, with China's accession to the WTO, this will likely change, and the business community needs to develop a set of business ethics to take advantage of the opportunity. Socialist ideology cannot help, for it has no room for commercial activities. Confucianism, another powerful worldview in China, has no ideological foundation for business ethics in the contemporary world.

China has many people who have a lot of business experience, and the country's university-level MBA programs are flourishing. There is no lack of basic business knowledge, but a vacuum exists in business ethics. This involves social values, worldviews, and even metaphysics—areas that are beyond current classroom studies. An ethical system touches upon a society's core values and may even define its civilization. This approach will certainly challenge the ideological foundation of China's state orthodoxy. Currently, government leaders are aware that the society lacks a viable intellectual underpinning for economic growth, but they are yet to come to terms with the fact that socialism is a bankrupt ideology in this regard.

With 1.3 billion potential customers and an impressive track record of economic growth for more than 20 years, few places in the world are more attractive for commercial investment. Anyone serious about international business cannot ignore China or its economic impact on the world. China is largely an untapped market in the fields of finance, law, travel, and communication—fields that are fast coming to a saturation point in the developed countries. As China lowers its trade barriers, business people will flood in. There will also be intense competition between domestic enterprises and foreign companies, and among foreign investors. Anyone who can get there quickly will perhaps gain a firmer foothold and establish some dominance.

Holistic entrepreneurs, of course, face additional challenges.

These go beyond merely starting and maintaining businesses to exercising kingdom values, empowering the disadvantaged, and expanding the kingdom. Christian business endeavors need to build on the foundation of Christian beliefs and values. The theological assumption of stewardship interprets business as a call to be faithful with God's resources. Therefore, a Christian business person seeks not his or her gslory, but God's. The ultimate objective of Christian business is to glorify God through business activities. Financial gain is not the only criterion to judge a Christian business. Its ethical approach is at least as important as the bottom line. A Christian business ultimately belongs to God, not to the Christian entrepreneur. Through business activities, holistic entrepreneurs hope to witness to the values of the kingdom, including justice, honesty, fairness, humility, charity, integrity, and creativity.

Viable Christian businesses, first of all, can display relevant Christian values and the biblical worldview in the marketplace. Outstanding foreign business enterprises may even be able to further serve China by establishing industrial standards as the country opens for new markets and services. For decades, the Chinese government—as well as many Chinese intellectuals—looked at Christianity as irrelevant to the country's progress. They have seen the Christian faith as a set of moral precepts, but not as a dynamic force in a competitive commercial world. The government is aware that Christianity, like Confucianism or socialism, can make a moral contribution to society. However, Confucianism and socialism—the two moral systems that the Chinese government has keyed in on—have little to say about business ethics. Buddhism and Daoism, too, are nearly silent on this topic. The folk religion still prevalent in some parts of China is no help, as it emphasizes fatalism and superstition.

Therefore, a successful Christian business can be a powerful witness for the validity of the Christian faith in modern society. Furthermore, Christian ethics, through business practices, might be incorporated into the new Chinese social ethics should the government regard them as a viable option for China. It is an unprecedented opportunity for Christians to influence China profoundly by exercising kingdom values.

Second, Christian business entrepreneurs can use their resources and talents to empower people who live in developing areas. Although the returns on their investments may not compare with those in more prosperous areas, Christians should take note of several other factors. These regions are generally open to business people, but are usually restricted to others. Christian business people can witness to their faith in places others cannot go. Various geographical barriers often isolate people in these poor regions, and the act of investing there is in itself a powerful message of God's care. From a practical standpoint, these areas often have less competition for investors. There may well be ample opportunities for economic development, but inhabitants may lack critical know-how, capital, or the market that can be provided by the investor. Finally, by economically empowering the people in these regions, Christians can help to build a more just society, which is a part of the gospel message in its living form.

Third, as this book documents, many Chinese Christian business people are already doing a marvelous job. International holistic entrepreneurs can team up synergistically. Chinese business people know the terrain and have good connections. Foreign entrepreneurs are versed in the world market, have access to capital, and possess the know-how. Both partners can learn much from each other, both by exchanging business knowledge and through spiritual interaction. Such partnership will bring out the best of both worlds and can produce a rewarding relationship and an ideal team spirit.

Finally, Great Commission Christians cannot ignore the fact that China and its surrounding trading partner countries are inside the 10/40 Window and are mostly "closed" to traditional missionaries. Yet they are open to merchants, especially Chinese merchants. Many of the peoples in this sphere of business influence are Muslims and Buddhists—two of the most difficult-to-reach groups.

As China has embarked on the road to a market economy, it has become one of the most economically successful countries in Asia. Trade is increasing between China and these surrounding nations, most of them former communist states, from Myanmar to Mongolia and from North Korea to Cambodia. Many of these countries are also copying China's economic reform policies. If Christian business enterprises can demonstrate successful track records in China, they may also establish a business paradigm and the credentials to be welcomed by these formerly restricted countries.

There are already Christian business people, many from Wenzhou, doing business holistically in these countries. They can penetrate the most politically inaccessible areas of the world, because China now has virtually no enemies. If overseas Christian business leaders can join hands with Chinese Christian merchants, together they may be able to share the gospel thr ough business activities in strategic locations. China may, one day, become a powerhouse to send out missionaries, in various unconventional forms, to proclaim the kingdom. We may soon read a new chapter in mission history as God, through business development in China, proclaims his kingdom even beyond its boundaries.

Appendix

Appendix: Resource Materials

Hundreds of volumes on doing business in China are available. Unfortunately, most of them are outdated as soon as they appear because of rapidly changing developments on China's business landscape. Numerous volumes on legal and regulatory issues on China, constantly updated, are also available. For those who are just starting out in this field, the following resources should prove helpful.

One of the best one-volume introductions to China is Dick Wilson's *China: The Big Tiger—A Nation Awakes* (London: Abacus, 1997). It provides the overall context of China for nonspecialists in a fair and concise manner. Lawrence Brahm and Li Daoran's *The Business Guide to China* (Singapore: Naga China Investments Ltd., 1996) is a handy volume on technical matters, such as taxation law, joint ventures, copyright, foreign exchange, and investment. Although China's WTO entrance may soon make this book outdated, it still presents relevant background information. A good complementary book is *China Business: Context & Issues* (Hong Kong: Longman, 1995), edited by Howard Davie. This volume presents fine articles on "Business Ethics in China," "The Emergence of Retail Markets," "Accounting in China," and "The Natures of Firms." Davie's volume provides a thematic background to business issues in China.

Several other useful books will help newcomers. Ming-jer Chen's *Inside Chinese Business: A Guide For Managers Worldwide* (Boston: Harvard Business School Press, 2001) is a must for all serious Western readers who want to understand the business culture in China. Along the same lines, Scott D. Seligman's *Chinese Business Etiquette* (New York: Warner, 1999) is an extremely useful roadmap for the average Western business person to find ways through the Chinese protocol labyrinth. Seligman's book is a practical handbook to show Westerners how to build relationships with Chinese counterparts. It provides detailed instructions on such things as seating for a formal dinner, the fine arts of gift giving, and the correct way to address people.

There are various schools of thoughts of the future economy of China—from boom to bust. Callum Henderson's *China on the Brink: The Myths and Realities of the World's Largest Market* (New York: McGraw-Hill, 1999) provides a balanced view. The author interprets the Chinese economic scene from the context of the recent Asian financial crisis. He provides the fundamentals to understand China's political and economic dynamics. In the end, he demythologizes many popular notions on China in a rational and convincing manner. Except for his prediction that the Renminbi would be devalued, most of his short-term prognostications on China seem to be coming true. James Ogilvy, Peter Schwartz, and Joe Flower's *China's Future: Scenarios for the World's Fastest Growing Economy, Ecology, and Society* (San Francesco: Jossey-Bass Inc., 2000) examines current socioeconomic trends and comes up with three different, yet possible, scenarios. These scenarios, presented in matrix form, can help business people to formulate strategic options and test them. As geoeconomic dynamics become more volatile, simulations and scenarios are becoming increasingly important business tools.

Oliver Yau and Henry Steels edited *China Business: Challenges in the 21st Century* (Hong Kong: Chinese University of Hong Kong Press, 1999). This volume publishes the latest academic research on cross-cultural management issues, China's stock market, importing foreign technology, and other themes. While it does a good job from a scholarly perspective, business practitioners may find it too abstract.

Chan Kwok Bun edited *Chinese Business Networks: State, Economy and Culture* (Singapore: Prentice Hall, 2000). It deals with business networks among the Chinese diaspora. However, like the previous volume, this one is aimed more at academicians than at business people.

Icapital Limited, the commercial arm of China's National Statistics Bureau (www.statchina.com), publishes different kinds of market data and regional economic statistics. If one is serious about a particular sector, region, or market, the information from this company is indispensable. However, be warned that its books are rather expensive.

For the latest developments in trade regulations and policies, check the Web site of the China Ministry of Foreign Trade and Economic Cooperation (www.moftec.gov.cn). It provides the latest trade regulation changes. This is important because China will rewrite and abolish as many as 5,000 trade and economic regulations because of its entry into the WTO. One can access all of the WTO documents on China at the www.wto.org site. However, these documents run thousands of pages. For a simplified presentation about the market potential of China's WTO accession, check the Hong Kong Government Trade Development Council's site for its WTO booklet at www.tdctrade.com/wto/tid.htm.

One of the best magazines to stay updated is the weekly *Far Eastern Economic Review*. It is an indispensable tool for any business practitioner in China, reporting the latest business trends on Asia in general and on China in particular. The *Asian Wall Street Journal* and the *South China Morning Post* provide excellent business reports on China on a daily basis. The most informative Web site is www.china.org.cn, operated by the government. It offers the latest news and official regulations in several major languages. For those who read Chinese, the best site is the www.sina.com.cn. It carries a massive business and finance section that covers news in practically all sectors and all regions in China with real-time updates. It also has a large archive.

Finally, Hoong Yik Luen's *New China Rising: A Social Economic Assessment of WTO Entry* (Singapore: Private Publication, 2001, ISBN: 981-04-534-3) is perhaps the most reader-friendly volume among the hundreds of books available on China and the WTO. Loaded with insights, this book gives no-nonsense descriptions of the major economic themes in China. Busy executives and managers who want to understand China's business environment can get a good grasp in a short period of time with this extremely practical and insightful volume